Baby Quilts from Grandma

by Carolann M. Palmer

That Patchwork Place, Inc., Bothell, Washington

Baby Quilts from Grandma

Dedication

This book is dedicated to my three daughters: Carolee, Lorellen, and Janet, who are giving me reasons to write it; and to grandmothers, mothers, daughters, and aunts, who are looking for a special something to create and give to a very precious baby or child. Every baby needs to experience the love that bursts forth from a handmade quilt.

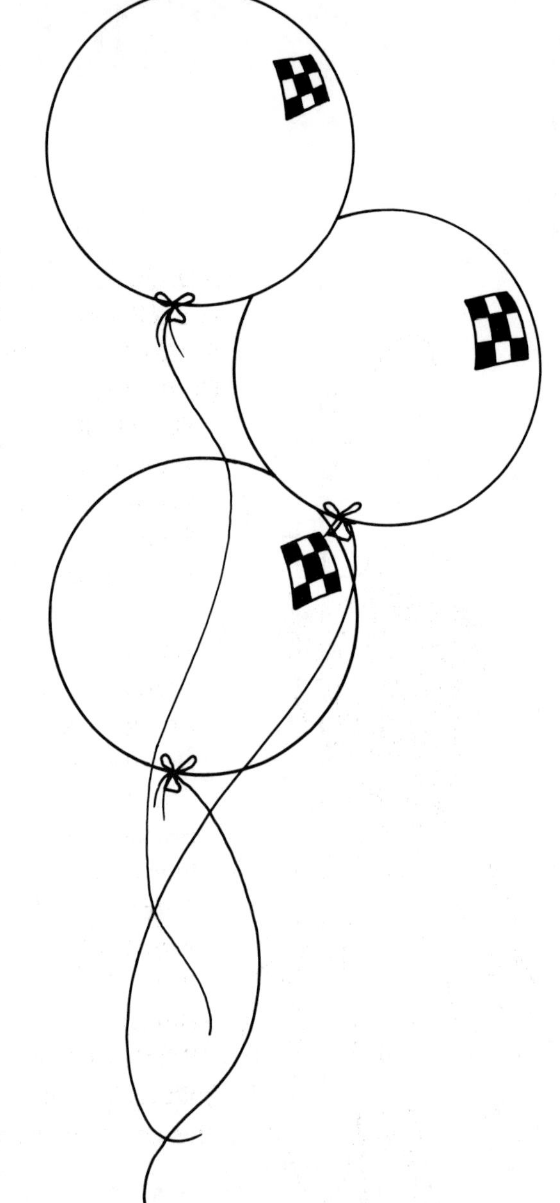

Acknowledgments

Special thanks to members of the Seattle Quilt Troupe and the Monday Night Bowling League, my two quilting groups, who gave encouragement, advice, and support in this project; and to Nancy Martin for her help and faith in me.

Thanks to my daughter, Jan Cote, for her illustration ideas.

Thank you to Heartland Interiors, located in Country Village, Bothell, Washington, for the loan of the painted furniture used in the photos.

Credits

Photography . . . . Carl Murray
Illustration and Graphics . . . . Stephanie Benson
Barbara Tourtillotte

Baby Quilts from Grandma©

© Carolann M. Palmer, 1988

No part of this book may be reproduced without permission of the publisher, That Patchwork Place, Inc., P.O. Box 118, Bothell, WA 98041.

Library of Congress Number: 88050424

ISBN: 0-943574-48-X

Contents

Introduction 4
Guidelines for Proper Planning 5
Rotary Cutting Techniques 8
Quilt Patterns 9
- Baby Rail 10
- Baby Twist 12
- Primary Nine-Patch 14
- Snowball 16
- Frilly Hearts 18
- Irish Bear Chain 20
- Anthony's Christmas Quilt 22
- Rainbow Trout 24
- Froggy, Froggy 26
- Duckyflies 37
- Rainbow Kites 40
- Box of Crayons 42
- Fishy, Fishy 44
- Cats 46
- Amish Mice 48
- Pussy Cats 50
- Bunny Lunch 52
- Whales in School 54

Quilting Terms 57
Glossary of Techniques 59

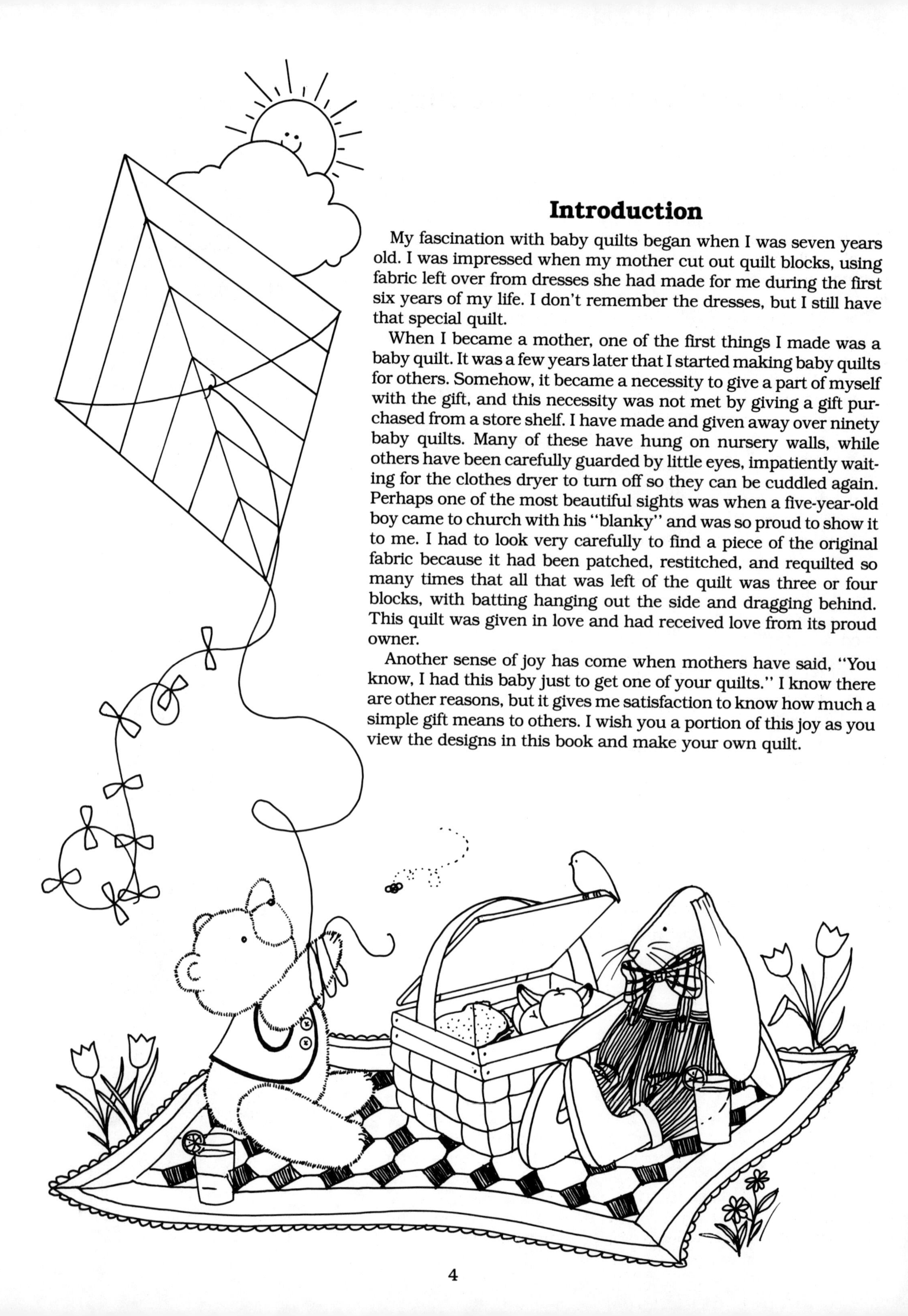

Introduction

My fascination with baby quilts began when I was seven years old. I was impressed when my mother cut out quilt blocks, using fabric left over from dresses she had made for me during the first six years of my life. I don't remember the dresses, but I still have that special quilt.

When I became a mother, one of the first things I made was a baby quilt. It was a few years later that I started making baby quilts for others. Somehow, it became a necessity to give a part of myself with the gift, and this necessity was not met by giving a gift purchased from a store shelf. I have made and given away over ninety baby quilts. Many of these have hung on nursery walls, while others have been carefully guarded by little eyes, impatiently waiting for the clothes dryer to turn off so they can be cuddled again. Perhaps one of the most beautiful sights was when a five-year-old boy came to church with his "blanky" and was so proud to show it to me. I had to look very carefully to find a piece of the original fabric because it had been patched, restitched, and requilted so many times that all that was left of the quilt was three or four blocks, with batting hanging out the side and dragging behind. This quilt was given in love and had received love from its proud owner.

Another sense of joy has come when mothers have said, "You know, I had this baby just to get one of your quilts." I know there are other reasons, but it gives me satisfaction to know how much a simple gift means to others. I wish you a portion of this joy as you view the designs in this book and make your own quilt.

Guidelines for Proper Planning

Choosing the Design

A baby quilt can be a simple, quick project, and most of the designs in this book can be completed in a short time. Look carefully at the designs that appear to be more complex and you will see that they really are easily put together. Some designs are traditional, while others are contemporary. Modern tools and speed-cutting and speed-piecing techniques will make your baby quilt a joy to make, give, and use.

One of the first things to consider in making a baby quilt is to determine its intended purpose. Obviously, it is for a baby. But will it be part of the room decoration and hang on a wall, or is it to be loved and used? What color is the nursery? Does it need to match an existing color scheme or particular print? Rooms can be designed around a print in the quilt, or the quilt can be geared to the room design.

If the baby has already arrived, then you can choose a color or design that is more appropriate. For instance, a ruffled edge is more frequently seen on a little girl's quilt, and the quilt would generally be made with lighter colors and perhaps eyelet or lace, whereas a boy's quilt may have darker colors and a straight binding.

In choosing a pattern, you may wish to consider nursery decor, parents' life-style, whether the baby is a boy or girl, or if a traditional or contemporary design would be more welcome. Another factor is the time element. If you want to make a quilt in a short period of time, choose one of the new speed-cutting and speed-piecing techniques. Then tie, rather than quilt it. Or you may want to make a baby quilt any color, pattern, or way you wish just for the fun of it. A look through this book will show many ways of making a truly fine quilt in a short period of time.

Fabric Selection

It only takes one trip to the quilt shop to see that there are many fabrics from which to choose. The easiest fabric to work with is 100% cotton. Modern technology has improved the quality of cotton today to make it more durable, softer, and easier to work with. Prints are coordinated, sometimes making it difficult to choose which ones to use. Be sure to have a variety of prints in your selection. Include large prints as well as small prints, stripes, and dots. Texture will add an important part to your quilt. Novelty prints can also be used for special effects. For instance, when looking for "eyes" for the animal designs, I found a print with large polka dots that looked like they had been swirled on with paint. Look carefully at dress material for a specialized look. However, to avoid odd looks, it is not necessary to reveal that you are looking for "fish eyes."

Color

Color is one of the most important design elements in a quilt. You can vary the look of a quilt so much by choosing different colors and by putting colors in different places on each block. Soft pastels or light colors lend a delicate, soft look, while dark or more intense colors have a more solid look. The use of primary colors tends to excite and stimulate baby eyes, while softer tones quiet and soothe. Consider these elements when deciding on color.

Helpful Tools

Any project is as good as the tools used to make it. If quilting is a new adventure for you, consider investing in a few tools to make this process easier.

Scissors

You will need two pairs of scissors. One pair will be used for making accurate templates and cutting paper patterns, and the other pair only for cutting fabric. If necessary, put a padlock on the handles of your good scissors, so the rest of the family will leave them alone, or hide them in a secret place.

Rotary Cutter and Mat

The accuracy and speed of this device is well worth its price. You will need a cutter, mat, and straight edge. I cut almost all my quilts with this aid and can barely remember life without it. More and more patterns are being written with rotary instructions. It is easy to use and very accurate.

Ruler

A transparent ruler is invaluable to a quilter. It is marked in 1/8″ segments, and lines can be drawn smoothly and accurately. An 18″ ruler is a must and the thicker 24″ x 6″ one is great for use with the rotary cutter.

Pins

One nice thing to do for yourself is to throw away your short, dull pins and get a new box of quilters' pins. These pins are 1 3/4″ long, strong, and helpful for pinning multiple layers of fabric, especially when basting a quilt.

Needles

Long, soft sculpture needles are great for basting a quilt, while "betweens" are recommended for applique and quilting.

Thimble

Find a well-fitting thimble. If you haven't already, now is the time to learn to use one, to avoid holes in fingertips and to help maintain sanity.

Markers

Although there is controversy over the long-term effects, the invention of the water erasable marker is a boon to quilters. It works like a felt pen, comes in several colors, and will disappear when sprayed or washed in cold water. Certain pencils also work well. Test all markers and pencils following manufacturer's directions before using.

Masking Tape

Masking tape in several sizes is good for marking straight lines. The 1/4″ size is ideal for quilting exactly 1/4″ from a seam line. The 1″ width is very helpful when making mitered corners.

Ironing Board and Iron

A standard steam iron and board are fine for quilting. However, consider making your own ironing board if you sew a lot. Determine how much room you have, then buy an unfinished door to fit the space. A 36″ x 72″ door is a nice size to use. Drill a number of holes for ventilation; then cover with an old mattress pad and muslin, stretching to make the top smooth, and tack it to the back. It really helps to have a large padded surface to iron 45″ or 60″ material in one sweep. It also makes a fine surface on which to pin pieces of a block when deciding which fabrics to use. This board could be stored in a closet when not in use.

Sewing Machine

A sewing machine in good repair is the cornerstone to quilting. It need not be the latest design. Keep the needles sharp and change them frequently. Know your machine and master how it works. Determine the guidelines for a 1/4″ seam on both sides of the needle and mark with masking tape if necessary.

Getting Started

You have the proper tools and materials; you have chosen the pattern and fabric. Now what? First, be sure to preshrink all fabric in a basin of hot water to make sure all dye residue is removed. Rinse until water is clear. Then dry fabric and press.

Most directions in this book use the rotary cutter instead of templates to cut each piece. Cut fabric according to directions. Make an accurate cardboard or plastic template if called for. Accuracy at this stage is one of the most important parts of quiltmaking. To be off even 1/16″ grows to 1″ every 16″, and that can cause problems if your quilt is 82″ long.

When sewing pieces together, press each seam before adding another one that crosses it. Press toward the darker fabric or away from where you will quilt. It will make the quilting easier and will also save time later if you know at this point just where you will quilt.

Rotary Cutting Techniques

One of the most valuable quilting tools is the rotary cutter. Long strips of fabric can be cut quickly, accurately and easily. The strips are then subcut into squares and triangles, eliminating the use of templates. Directions for the quilts in this book are written using this tool. If using a rotary cutter for the first time, follow the manufacturer's safety precautions. Using the following instructions will help you get started. You will need a rotary cutter, self-healing mat, and straight edge, available at your local quilt shop.

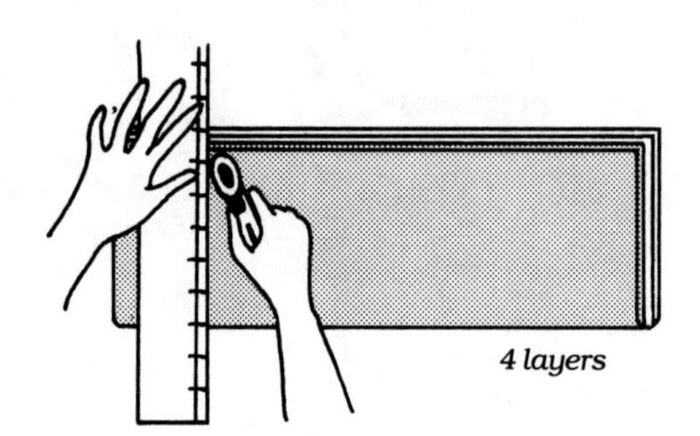
4 layers

1. Preshrink and press fabric like it comes off the bolt. Fold once more, lengthwise. You now have four layers.

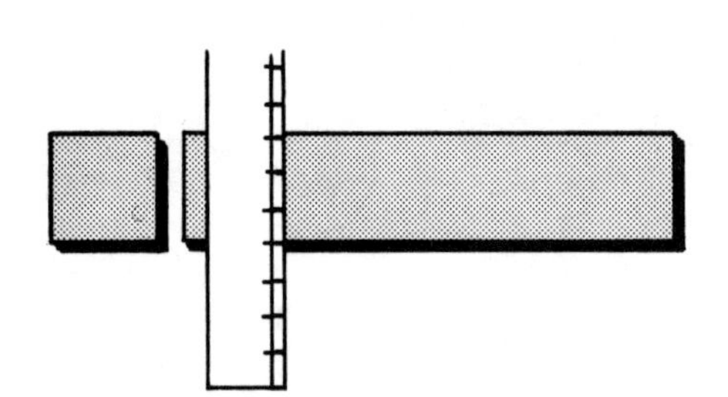

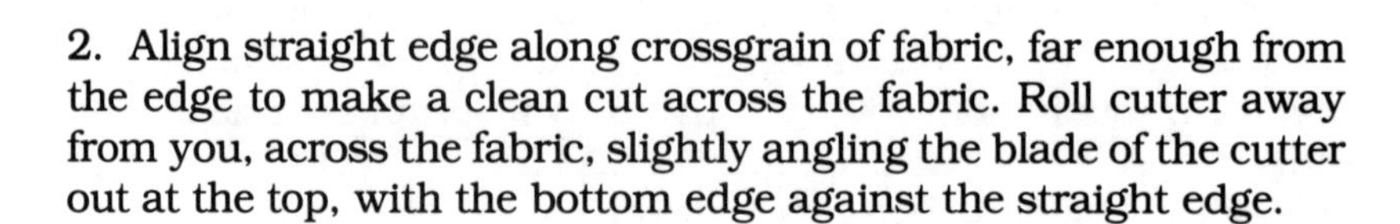
2. Align straight edge along crossgrain of fabric, far enough from the edge to make a clean cut across the fabric. Roll cutter away from you, across the fabric, slightly angling the blade of the cutter out at the top, with the bottom edge against the straight edge.

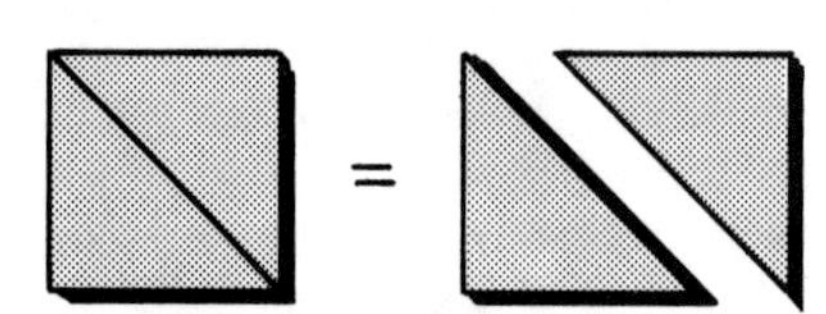
Cut diagonally for triangles

3. Cut fabric into strips, according to the measurement given; then subcut the strip into squares the width of the strip. Some directions say to cut in squares, then cut diagonally for triangles. Other directions say to cut twice diagonally for triangles.

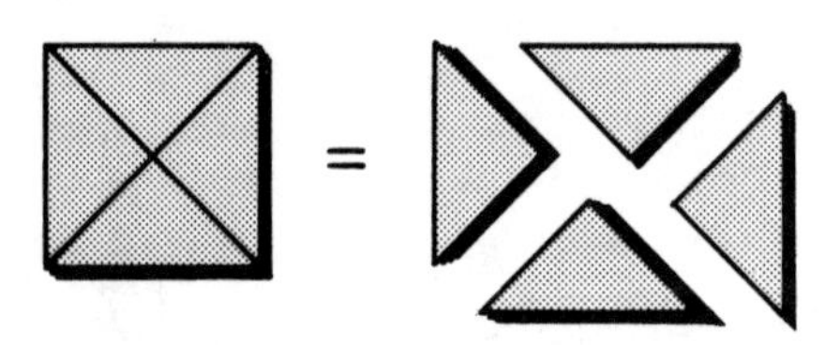
Cut twice diagonally for triangles

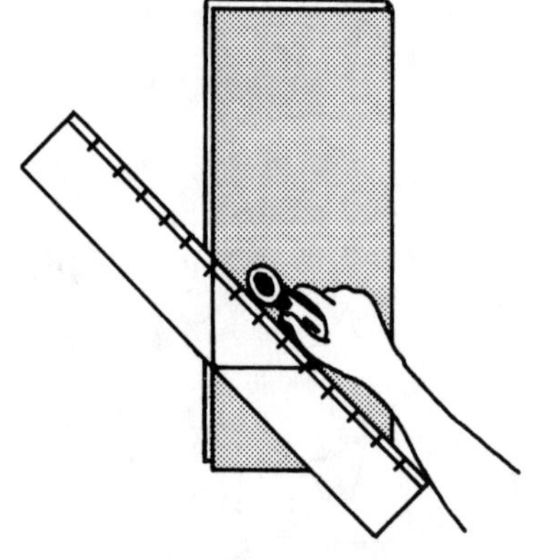
Align ruler at 45° angle for bias cut

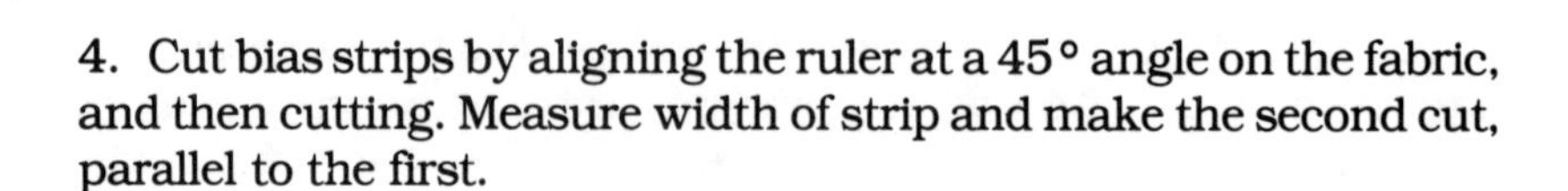
4. Cut bias strips by aligning the ruler at a 45° angle on the fabric, and then cutting. Measure width of strip and make the second cut, parallel to the first.

If the position of the fabric or straight edge is uncomfortable to you, reverse it. You should not feel like a pretzel or stand on your head to rotary cut. Practice on some scrap fabric and you soon will have this technique mastered.

Quilt Patterns

This section of the book contains directions and patterns for eighteen quilts of similar size. Partially shaded line drawings accompany each quilt design. You may use these as a worksheet and color in your own color scheme in the unshaded areas.

Many of the directions tell you to cut strips of fabric, then subcut into squares and cut the squares diagonally to form triangles. This speed-cutting technique is not only fast, but helps make more accurate triangles. Refer to page 8 for general rotary cutting techniques.

Templates are identified by quilt name and template number or letter. Cutting directions give number of pieces to cut from each fabric. Several templates are labeled A and AR, which means to cut a specified number like the template, then flip the template over and cut specified R or reversed pieces.

Fabric colors refer to the sample quilt. Refer to the color picture and then change colors if you wish.

All templates include a 1/4″ seam allowance as do the border cutting dimensions, except where noted. Grain line is noted where needed. Several templates are printed with a fold line. Be sure to make these templates full size before cutting the fabric. In some cases, smaller pieces overlap larger pieces, so be sure to include the entire template, including the space covered by the smaller piece, when you make the larger templates.

Several patterns use letter or number designations and are cut from given dimensions, rather than providing templates. DO NOT ADD SEAM ALLOWANCE. The correct cutting size is given in the directions.

Most borders are mitered. Multiple borders are sewn together in long strips and treated as one border before mitering.

The quilts are designed to use a 45″ wide fabric for backing. Since fabric width varies with each bolt of fabric, make sure you have a wide enough piece before basting. On most of the quilts, I've tried to stay within the 42-44″ range. Many blocks are interchangeable, and the quilts may be tied or quilted by hand or machine.

There is a list of quilting terms and a Glossary of Techniques on pages 57 to 62 that give directions on applique, mitered borders, and completing the quilt top, along with directions for pinning, basting, quilting, and binding your quilt into a finished project.

Baby Rail

Color photo on page 35.

This quilt is an excellent one for a non-quilter or for a "first" quilt. Using speed-piecing techniques and tying, instead of quilting, you can have this quilt ready to give in five short hours. Blocks form a weaving pattern, or you may choose to arrange them for your own design. In any case, this quilt is truly easy to make and will delight any new mother and baby.

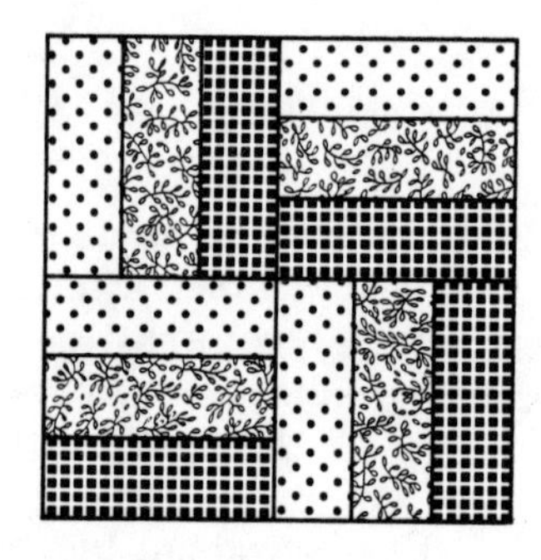

Baby Rail, four 6" pieced blocks.

Size: 44" x 50"

Materials: 45" wide fabric
1 1/4 yd. light for blocks and second border
1 yd. medium for blocks and binding
1 yd. dark for blocks and first border
1 1/2 yds. for backing
45" x 60" baby quilt batting
1 skein embroidery floss for tying

Cutting: Strips are approximately 45" long, cut from selvage to selvage.

From light:
- 7 strips, 2 1/2" wide, for blocks
- 5 strips, 3 1/2" wide, for second border

From medium:
- 7 strips, 2 1/2" wide, for blocks
  Cut remaining fabric into 2 1/2" bias strips for binding.

From dark:
- 7 strips, 2 1/2" wide, for blocks
- 5 strips, 1 1/2" wide, for first border

Sewing:
1. Sew one light, medium, and dark strip together on long sides. Cut into 6 segments, each 6 1/2" long. Repeat with remaining 6 sets of strips, making 42 Baby Rail blocks, each 6 1/2" x 6 1/2".

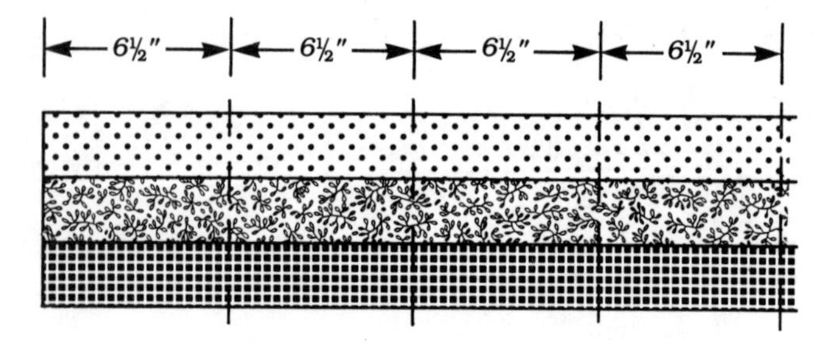

2. Arrange blocks as in block piecing guide above to make a zigzag pattern. Sew in rows and join rows for top as shown in quilt diagram on page 11.
3. Sew ends of 3 1/2" strips together to make 1 long strip. Repeat for 1 1/2" strips. Join long sides of these together for border.
4. Sew borders to quilt top according to directions in Glossary of Techniques on page 59.
5. Position backing, batting, and top. Pin, baste, quilt or tie, and bind according to directions in Glossary of Techniques on pages 60-61.

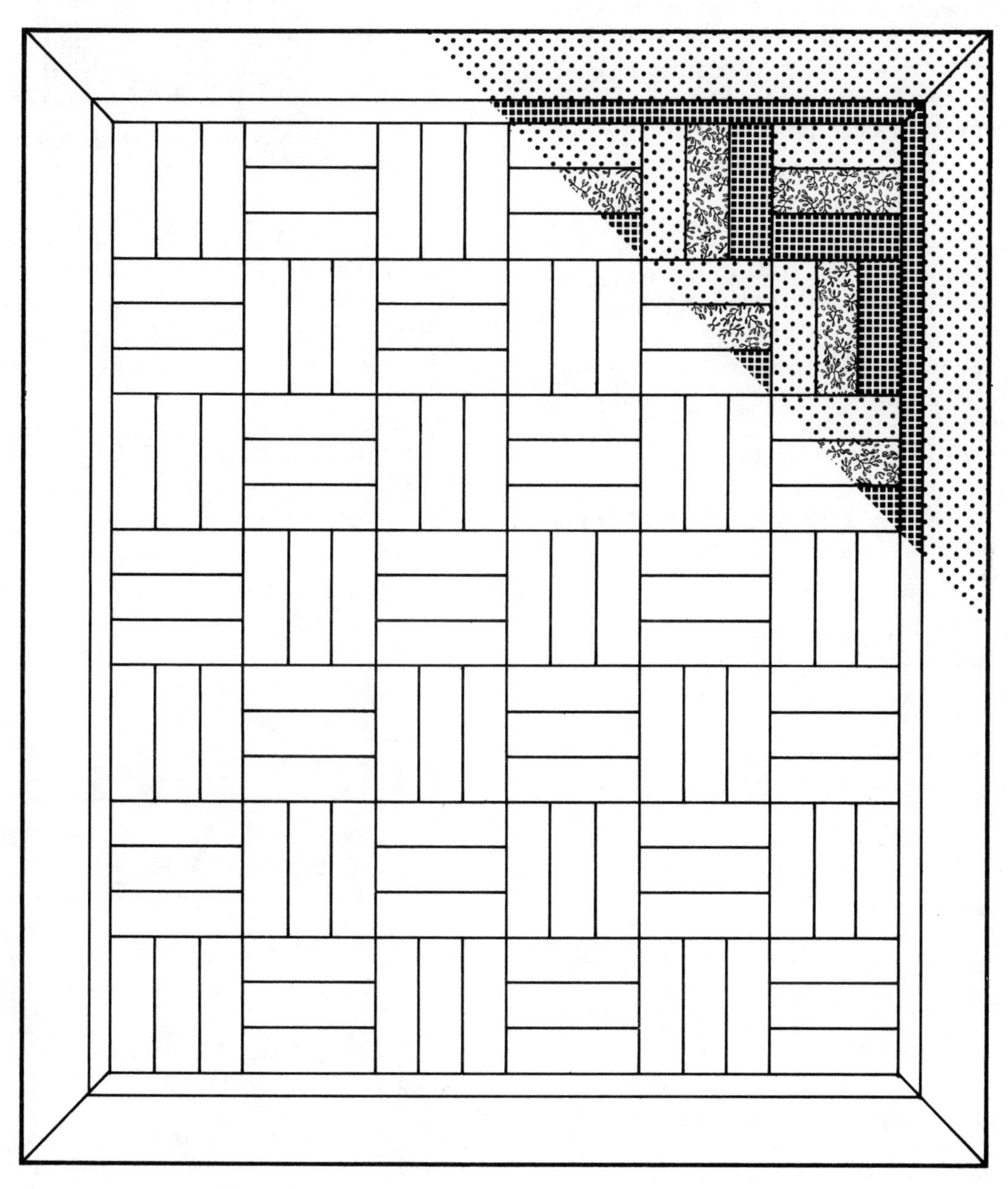

Baby Rail, 44″ x 50″

Baby Twist

Color photo on page 34.

This is another simple quilt to put together. The blocks can be set several different ways to make lots of movement for baby eyes to follow. Give yourself a treat by arranging the blocks in different ways before sewing the rows together. The weaving effect in the simple design makes it look complex. Be prepared for compliments on this one.

Size: 44″ x 50″

Materials: 45″ wide fabric
1 1/4 yds. A, light print for twist and second border
1 1/4 yds. B, medium print for twist and binding
1/2 yd. C, dark print for centers and first border
1 1/2 yds. for backing (If fabric is less than 44″ wide, purchase an additional 1/4 yd. and piece backing.)
45″ x 60″ baby quilt batting

Cutting: Strips are approximately 45″ long, cut from selvage to selvage.

From A:
10 strips, 2 1/2″ wide, for twist
Subcut into 84 pieces, 4 1/2″ long.
5 strips, 3 1/2″ wide, for second border
From B:
10 strips, 2 1/2″ wide, for twist
Subcut into 84 pieces, 4 1/2″ long.
From remaining fabric, cut 2 1/2″ bias strips for binding.
From C:
3 strips, 2 1/2″ wide
Subcut into 42 squares, 2 1/2″, for block centers.
5 strips, 1 1/2″ wide, for first border

Sewing:
1. Sew a dark center to medium rectangle with a half seam.

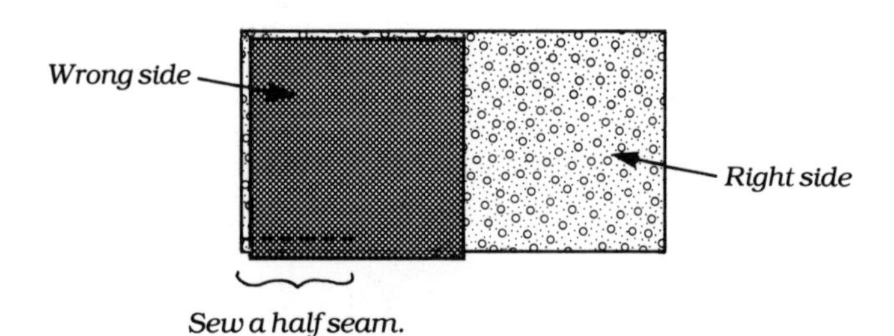

Sew a half seam.

Baby Twist, four 6″ pieced blocks.

2. Sew a light, medium, and light rectangle around center square, finishing with the remaining half seam. Make 42 blocks.

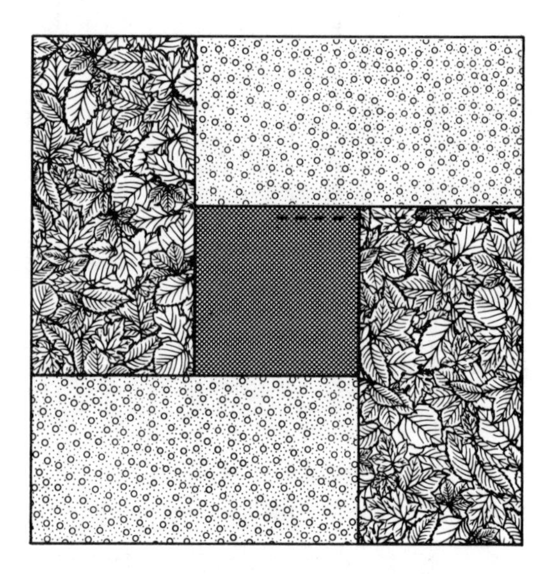

3. Sew blocks into rows in desired setting. Join rows for top as shown in quilt diagram on page 13.
4. Sew short ends of first border strips together. Repeat for second border strips. Join long sides of these strips together to make 1 long strip.
5. Press and sew borders to top as described in Glossary of Techniques on page 59.
6. Position backing, batting, and top. Pin, baste, quilt or tie, and bind according to directions in the Glossary of Techniques on pages 60-61.

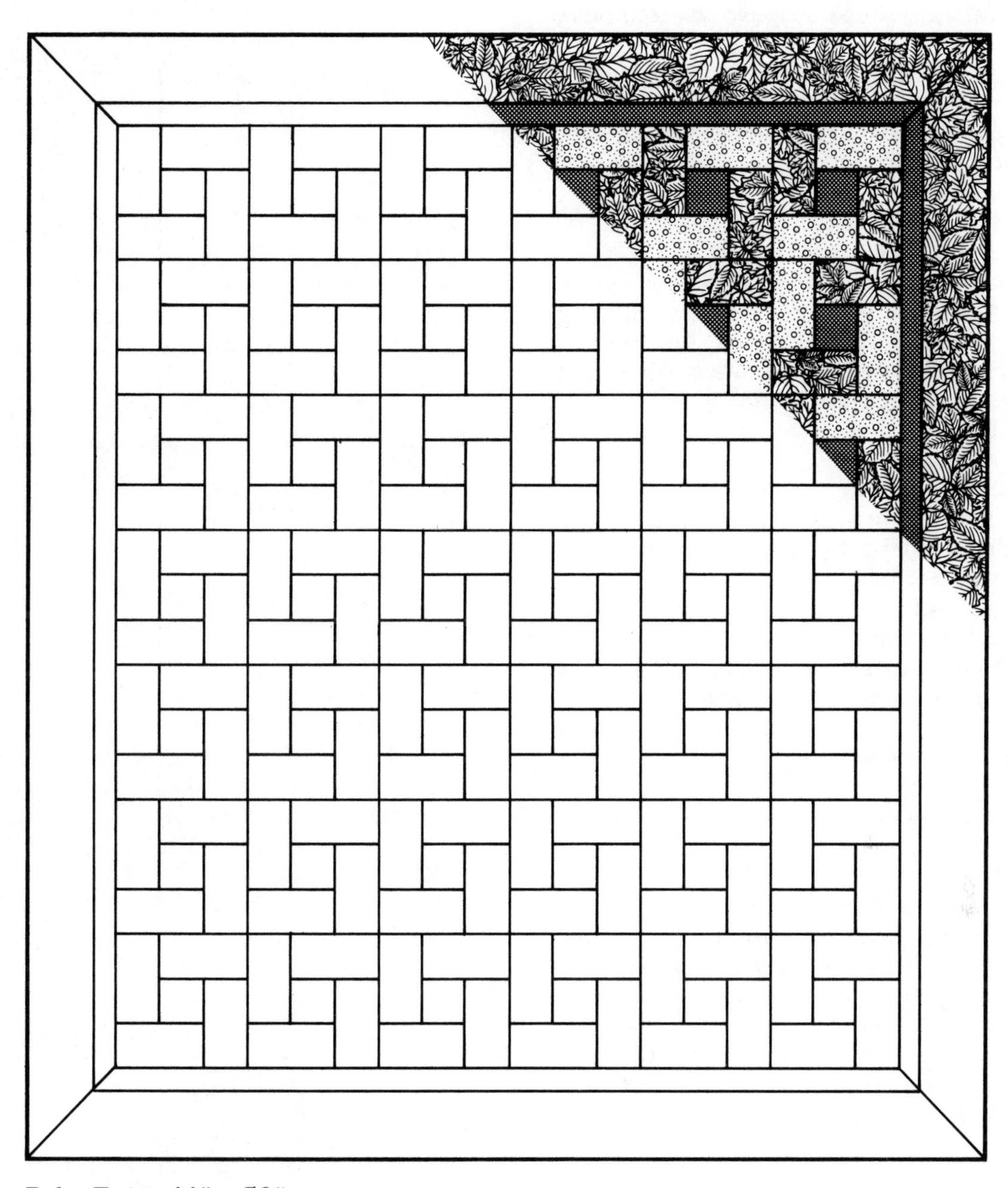

Baby Twist, 44″ x 50″

Primary Nine-Patch

Color photo on page 31.

The random placement of color makes this quilt come alive. Be adventurous in exploring color combinations and use a simple strip-piecing technique. It truly is painless.

Size: 42″ x 50″

Materials: 45″ wide fabric
1 1/4 yds. background
1/4 yd. each of 7 solid colors
3/8 yd. second border
1 1/2 yds. backing
45″ x 60″ baby quilt batting

Cutting: Strips are approximately 45″ long, cut from selvage to selvage.

From background:
15 strips, 2 1/2″ wide
Subcut 9 strips into 7 pieces, each 6 1/2″ long, for sashing and 6 strips into 3 pieces, each 14″ long for nine-patches.
From each of 7 solid colors:
3 strips, 2 1/2″ wide
Subcut 1 strip into 3 pieces, each 14″ long for nine-patches; 1 strip into 17 squares, 2 1/2″ x 2 1/2″ (5 for sashing and 12 for first border); save 1 strip for binding.
From second border fabric:
5 strips, 2 1/2″ wide

Sewing:
1. Make 20 Nine-patch blocks. Randomly choose color strips to sew with background to make 40 units of set 1 and 20 units of set 2. Sew a color strip to each side of 8 background strips for set 1. Sew a background strip to each side of 4 color strips for set 2. Cut each of these 12 units into 5 segments, 2 1/2″ long. Be sure to randomly choose colors. Sew these segments like this:

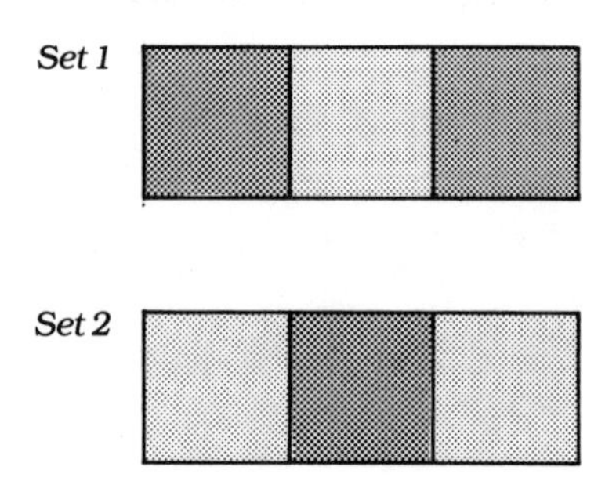

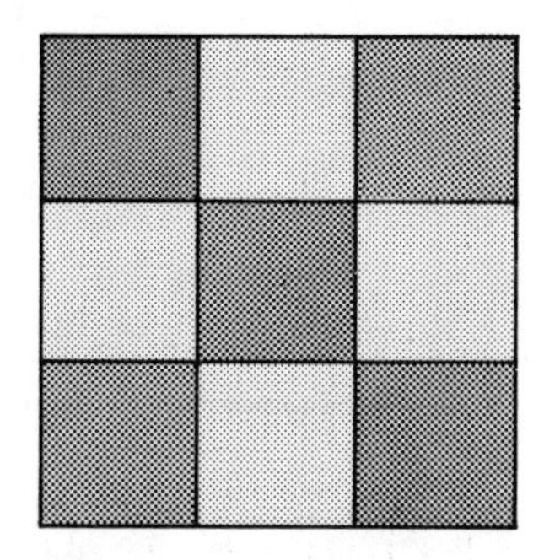

Nine-patch, 6″ block.

2. Sew 4 background sashing strips alternately with 5 random color squares, starting and ending with a square. Make 6 of these rows.
3. Sew 4 nine-patch blocks alternately with 5 sashing strips, starting and ending with sashing strip. Make 5 of these rows.
4. Sew these rows of nine-patch block rows and sashing alternately with sashing rows for quilt top, following quilt diagram on page 15.
5. Make first border strips by sewing 21 randomly selected 2 1/2″ solid squares for sides and 19 squares for top and bottom.
6. Sew second border strips to sides, top, and bottom of quilt, piecing where necessary.
7. Position backing, batting, and top. Pin, baste, and quilt according to directions in Glossary of Techniques on pages 60-61.
8. Make rainbow binding as follows: Sew binding strips as shown in diagram, beginning each strip 2″ lower than preceding one. Press to 1 side. Cut 2 1/2″ strips on bias from this piece. Join short ends into 1 long piece. Fold wrong sides together, matching raw edges, and press. Following directions in Glossary of Techniques on page 61, bind.

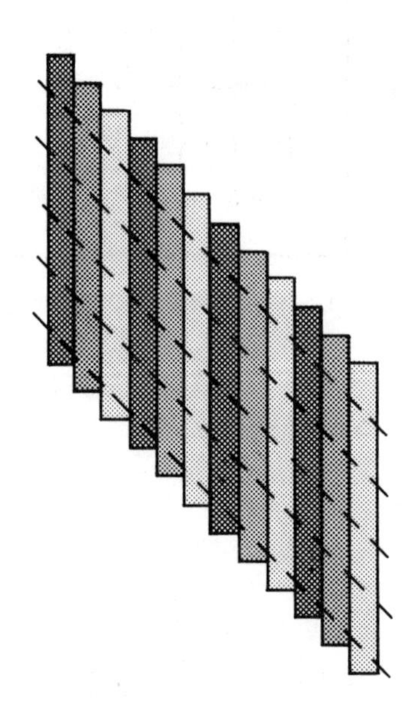

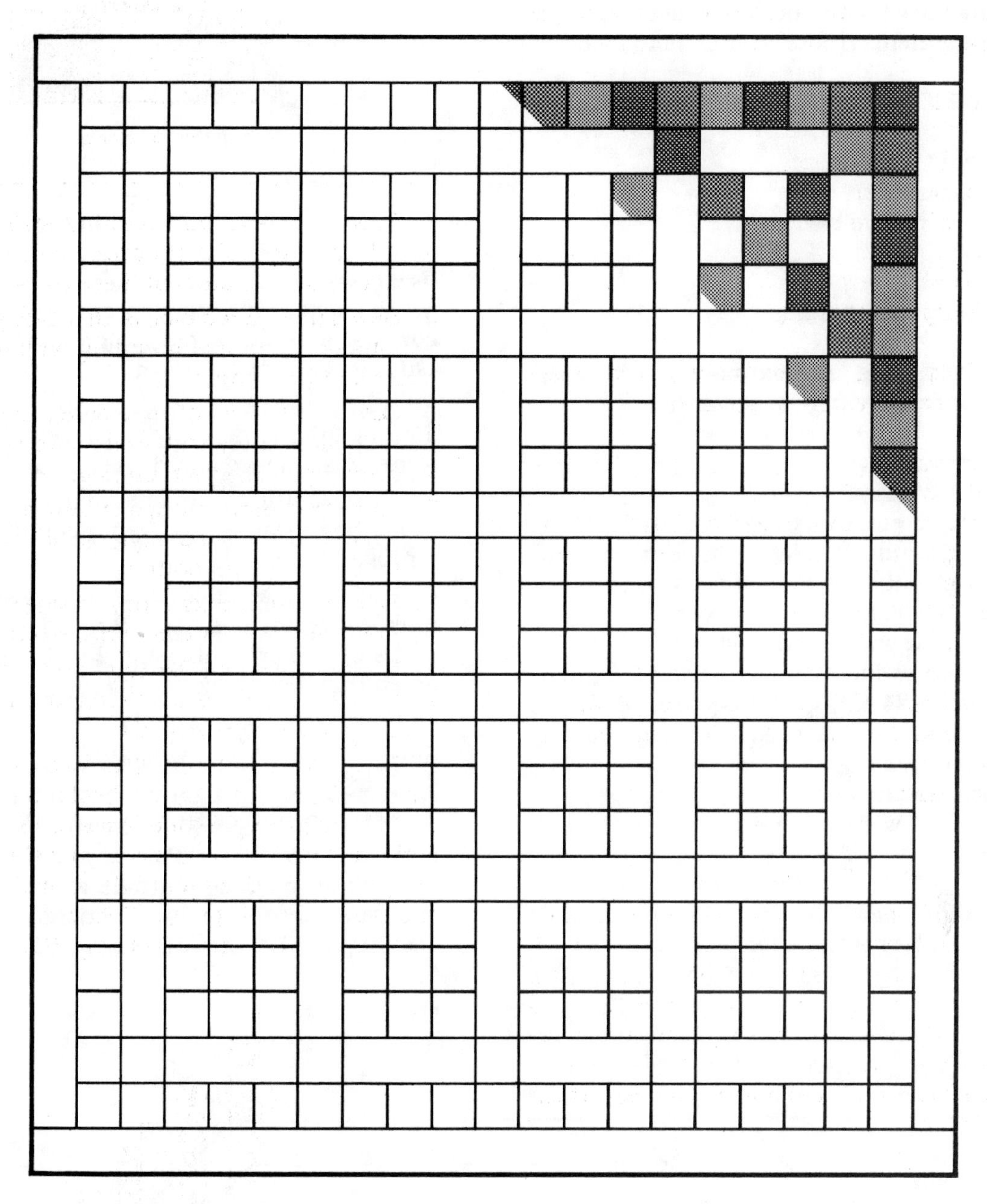

Primary Nine-Patch, 42″ x 50″

Snowball

Color photo on page 30.

Note how the block corners form another square, set on point, with a triangle of each color. This design is another one where you will want to try different block placements before sewing them together.

Size: 42″ x 53″

Materials: 45″ wide fabric
1 2/3 yds. background
1/3 yd. each of red, yellow, green
2/3 yd. blue
1 2/3 yds. backing
45″ x 60″ baby quilt batting

Cutting: Strips are approximately 45″ long, cut from selvage to selvage.

From background:
- 6 strips, 6 1/2″ wide
  - Subcut to 35 squares, 6 1/2″ x 6 1/2″. Position Cutting Template 1 in corner of each square and cut 4 corners off each square.
- 5 strips, 3″ wide, for second border

From red, yellow, green, and blue:
- 2 strips, 2 7/8″ wide
  - Subcut into 24 (26 green) squares, 2 7/8″ x 2 7/8″, then cut each square diagonally to make 48 triangles.

From red and green:
- 4 strips, 1 1/8″ wide, for first border

From yellow:
- 4 strips, 1 1/4″ wide for first border

From remaining blue:
- Cut into 2 1/2″ bias strips for binding.

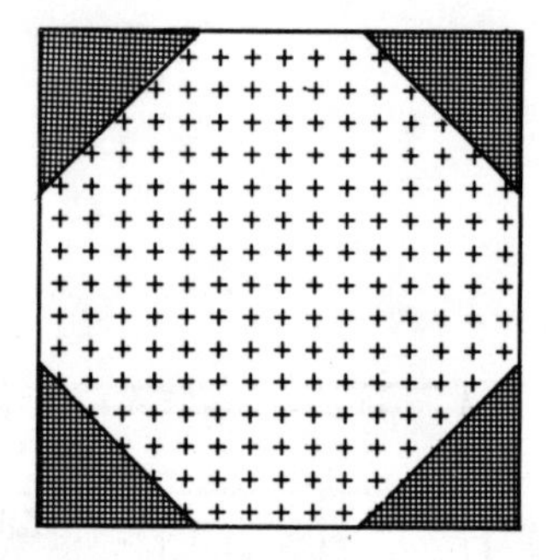

Snowball, 6″ block.

Sewing:

1. To background squares, add color triangles to 4 corners to make 11 red, 10 green, 7 yellow, and 7 blue blocks. Sew in rows and join rows as shown in quilt piecing guide.
2. Sew first border strips on long sides to make 4 strips in sequence of red, yellow, and green.
3. Using Cutting Template 2, cut strips to make 24 units, being careful to keep green on long side of template.
4. Add triangles to 2 corners of these 24 units to make 24 rectangles. Make 2 red, 4 green, 9 yellow, and 9 blue. Sew 2 blue and 2 yellow triangles to 4 green triangles for corner pieces.
5. Sew these border units together in color sequence as in quilt piecing guide.
6. Sew to top.
7. Sew second border strips to sides, then to top and bottom of quilt top.
8. Position backing, batting, and top. Pin, baste, and quilt according to directions in Glossary of Techniques on pages 60-61.

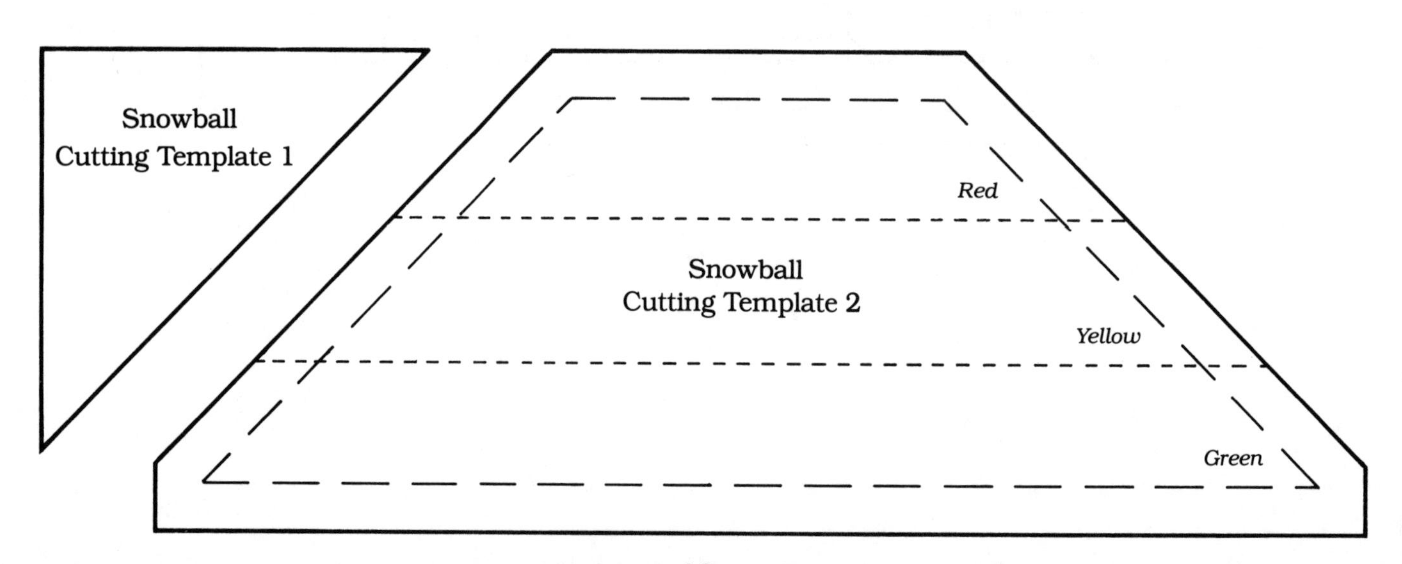

Snowball, 42″ x 53″

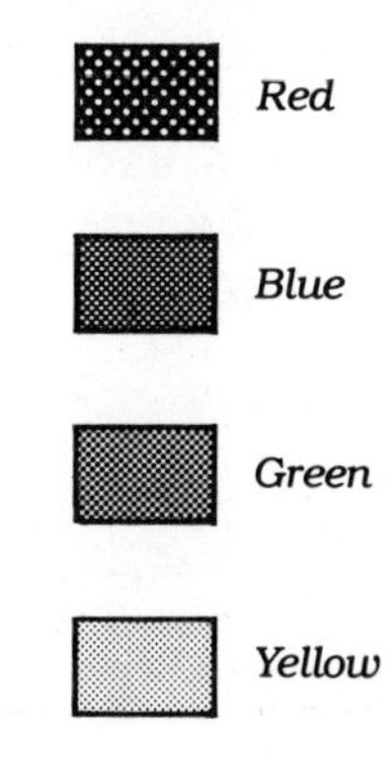

Frilly Hearts

Color photo on page 32.

The eyelet edging makes this quilt "frilly" and gives baby a textured surface to feel and rub. Color placement will add a lot to the additional diagonal design that forms when blocks are placed together. Be sure to use nondirectional fabric.

Size: 36″ x 48″

Materials: 45″ wide fabric
1 yd. light for background
2/3 yd. medium for blocks and second border
1 yd. dark for blocks, hearts, first and third borders
5 yds. of 3 ″ gathered eyelet
1 1/2 yds. backing
45″ x 60″ baby quilt batting

Cutting: Strips are approximately 45″ long, cut from selvage to selvage.

From light:
- 3 strips, 6 1/2″ wide
  - Subcut into 17 squares, 6 1/2″ x 6 1/2″, for applique blocks.
- 3 strips, 2 1/2″ wide, for pieced blocks

From medium:
- 6 strips, 2 1/2″ wide, for pieced blocks
- 5 strips, 2 1/2″ wide, for second border

From dark:
- 4 strips, 2 1/2″ wide, for pieced blocks
- 2 strips, 4″ wide, for hearts
  - Subcut into 17 squares, 4″ x 4″.

5 strips, 1″ wide, for first border
5 strips, 1 1/2″ wide, for third border

Sewing:
1. For pieced blocks, sew a light, medium, and dark strip, lengthwise. Make 2 1/2 strips of these. Cut crosswise into 36 segments, 2 1/2″ long.

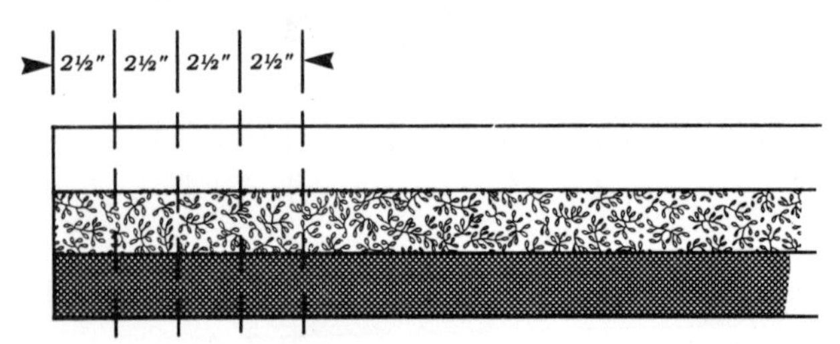

2. Sew a medium, dark, and medium strip, lengthwise. Make 1 1/2 strips. Cut crosswise into 18 segments, 2 1/2″ long.

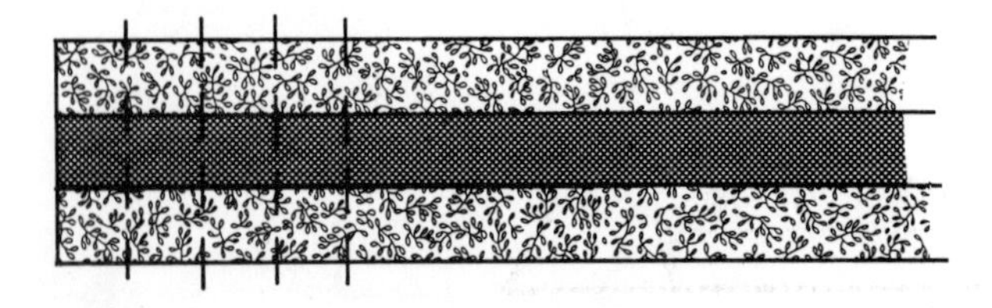

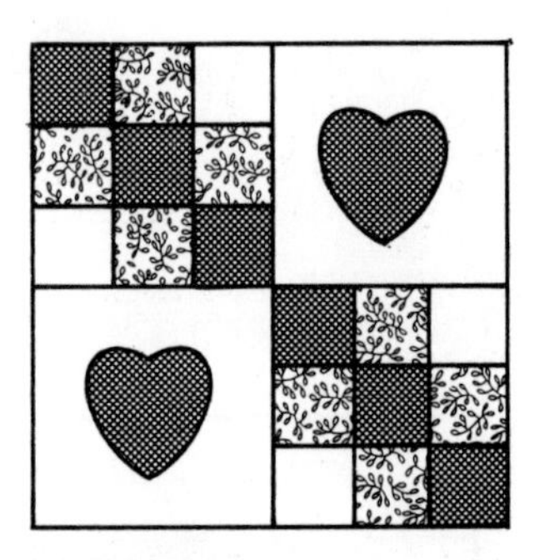

Frilly Hearts, 2 pieced and 2 applique blocks.

3. Sew to make 18 blocks.

4. Cut 17 hearts from paper. Cut 17 hearts plus 1/4″ seam allowance from dark squares. Paper-piece to light background according to directions in Glossary of Techniques on page 62.
5. Alternate pieced and applique blocks to form quilt top, following quilt piecing guide.
6. For borders, sew short ends of first border strips together. Repeat for second border strips. Join long sides of these strips together to make 1 long strip. Press and sew borders to top as described in Glossary of Techniques on page 59.
7. Stitch gathered eyelet to edge of quilt top, keeping raw edges even and gathering eyelet more at corners.

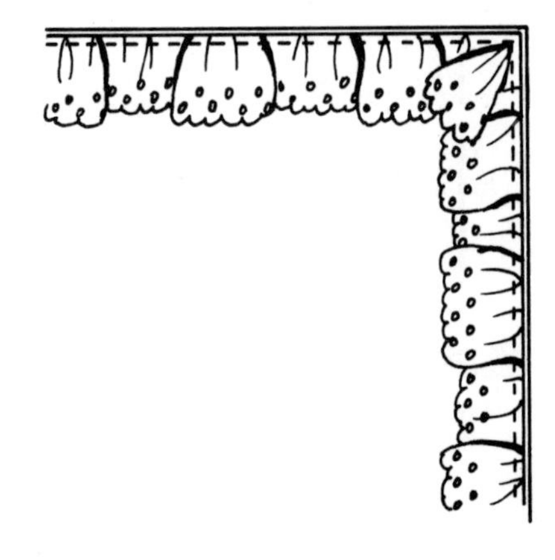

8. Position backing, batting, and top. Pin, baste, and quilt according to directions in Glossary of Techniques on pages 60-61.
9. Turn raw edges of top, eyelet, and backing to inside and blindstitch edge.

Frilly Hearts, 36″ x 48″

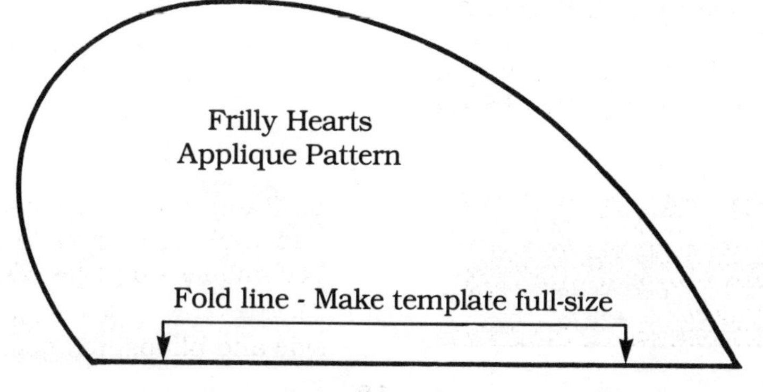

Irish Bear Chain

Color photo on page 33.

Press all seams toward dark colors and they will automatically fit together. This helps make quilting easier, especially on this quilt. Quilt bear pattern, found on page 38, into the center of each background block. Quilting in diagonal lines across the quilt top will help this quilt find its way to a crib a little faster.

Size: 42″ x 58″

Materials: 45″ wide fabric
1 1/3 yds. background
1 yd. light print for blocks
1 5/8 yds. dark print for blocks
1 2/3 yds. for backing
45″ x 60 ″ baby quilt batting

Cutting: Strips are approximately 45″ long, cut from selvage to selvage.

From background:
- 3 strips, 8″ wide
  - Subcut into 17 pieces, 5″ long.
- 2 strips, 5″ wide
- 4 strips, 2″ wide

From light print:
- 9 strips, 2″ wide
- 5 strips, 2 1/2″ wide

From dark print:
- 16 strips, 2″ wide
- 5 strips, 1″ wide
- Cut remaining fabric into 2 1/2″ wide bias strips.

Sewing:

1. Make 17, block A:

Sew 2″ wide dark strips to each long side of 5″ wide background strip. Repeat. Cut into 34 segments, each 2″ long.

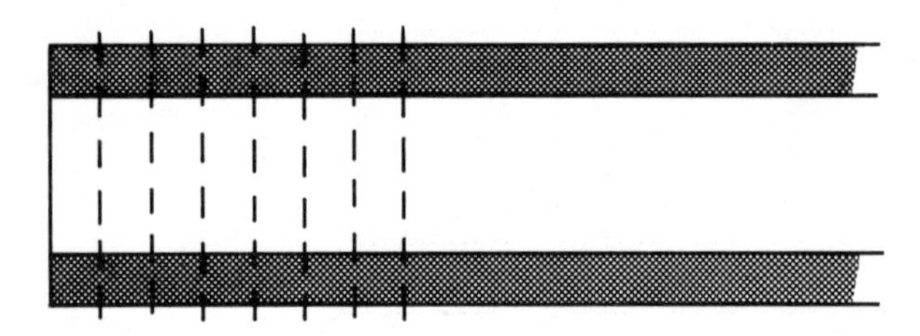

Join 2″ segments to each side of 5″ x 8″ background pieces.

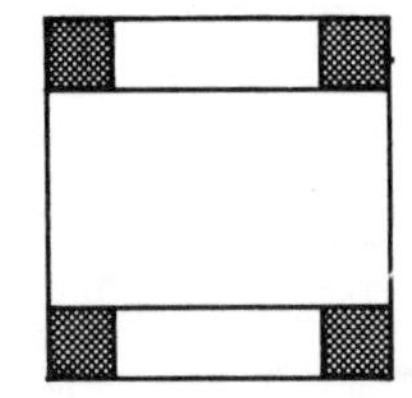

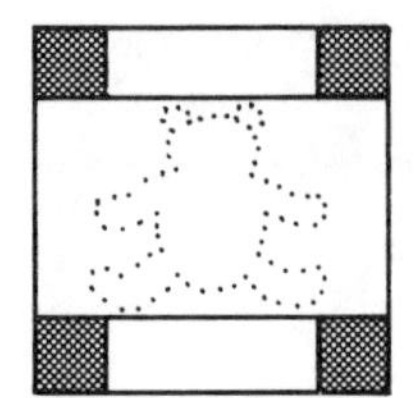

Block A, 7½″

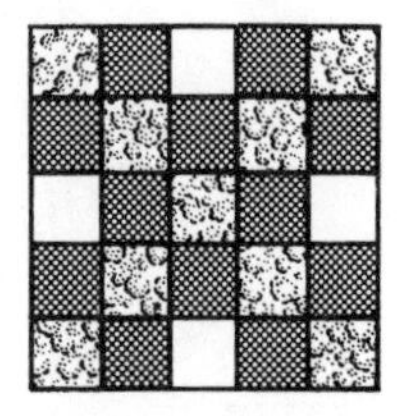

Block B, 7½″

2. Make 18, block B:

Using 2″ strips, sew 2 sets of Unit 1 and Unit 2. Cut into 36 segments, each 2″ long. Sew 1 set of Unit 3 and cut into 18 segments, each 2″ long. Following diagram above, join to make block.

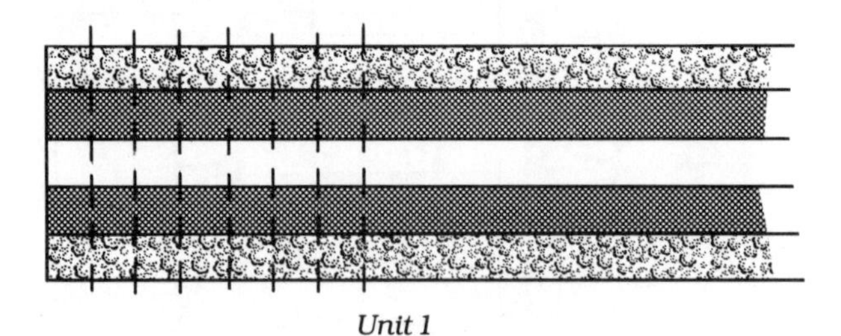

Unit 1

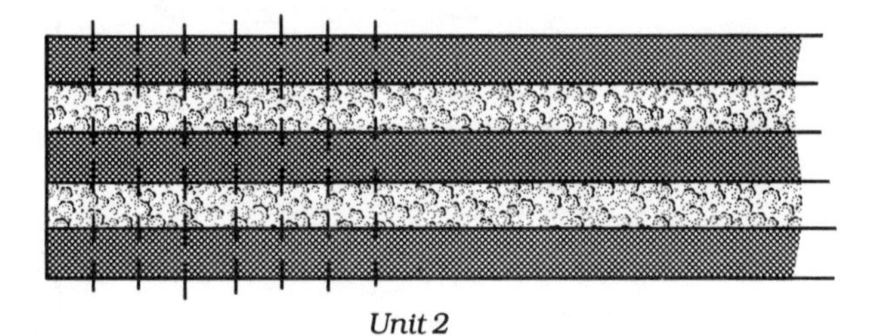

Unit 2

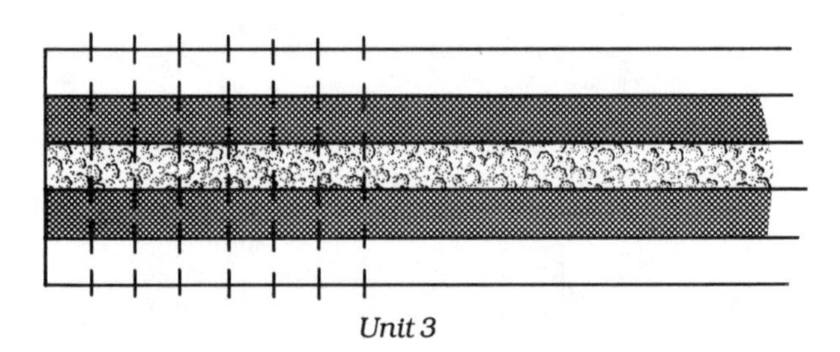

Unit 3

3. Following quilt diagram on page 21, join Blocks A and B alternately into rows, then join rows together to make quilt top.
4. For borders, join 1″ dark strips on short sides to make 1 long strip. Repeat for 2 1/2″ light print strips. Join long sides of these strips together to make 1 long strip. Press and sew borders to quilt top as described in Glossary of Techniques on page 59.
5. Position backing, batting, and top. Pin, baste, quilt, and bind according to directions in Glossary of Techniques on pages 60-61. Block A is quilted with the Bear quilting pattern found on page 38.

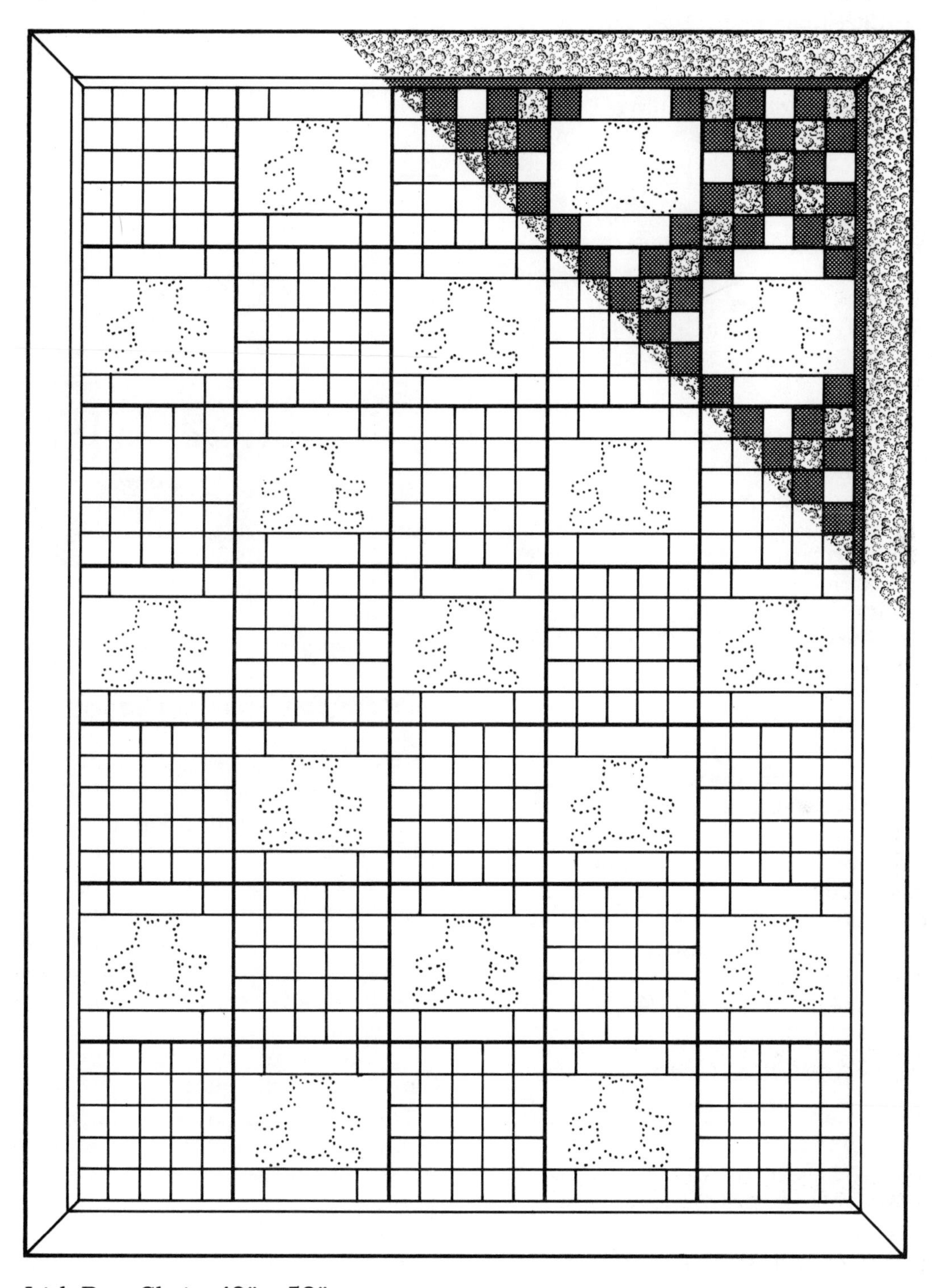

Irish Bear Chain, 42″ x 58″

Anthony's Christmas Quilt

Color photo on page 31.

Some families have a tradition that is linked to a specially made Christmas quilt. With great ceremony, on December 1, the "Christmas Quilt" is taken off the shelf and put on the bed, to be much looked at and handled during the month of December. The seasonal motifs help build anticipation for the coming holiday. Sometimes a pocket is placed somewhere on the quilt and magically is filled with candy or a small toy each day in December.

Being a new grandmother has made me aware of this tradition, which I want to keep alive by making and giving a special Christmas quilt to each of my grandchildren. This quilt is the first in this series.

Size: 54″ x 66″

Materials: 45″ wide fabric
1 1/4 yds. green print
1 1/4 yds. light background print
2 yds. red dot print
20 print squares with bear design
(at least 5″ square)
1-2 yds. striped print for borders (amount depends on number of repeats — about 300″ of identical border print is needed)
3 1/2 yds. for backing
58″ x 70″ quilt batting

Cutting: Strips are approximately 45″ long, cut from selvage to selvage.

From green print and light background print:
5 strips, 4 7/8″ wide
Subcut to 40 squares, 4 7/8″ x 4 7/8″, then cut diagonally to make 80 triangles.
3 strips, 5 1/4″ wide
Subcut to 20 squares, 5 1/4″ x 5 1/4″, then cut twice diagonally to make 80 triangles.
From red dot:
6 strips, 5 1/4″ wide
Subcut to 40 squares, 5 1/4″ x 5 1/4″, then cut twice diagonally to make 160 triangles.
7 strips, 1 1/2″ wide for first border
Cut 1/2 yd. into 2 1/2″ bias strips for binding.
From printed squares with bear designs:
20 squares, 4 1/2″ x 4 1/2″. Center bear on square.

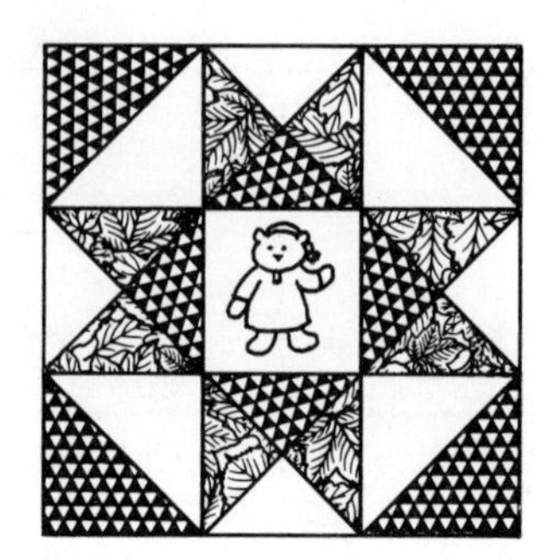

12″ block

Sewing:
1. Following diagram above, sew 20 blocks.
2. Following quilt diagram on page 23, sew blocks into rows and sew rows together to complete quilt top.
3. For striped print border, cut fabric lengthwise according to design and desired width, allowing 1/4″ on each side for seam allowance. Sew short ends together, matching print, to make 1 long strip.
4. Sew 1 1/2″ strips for first border together on short sides to make 1 long strip, then sew long edges to striped print border strip. Press and sew borders to top as described in Glossary of Techniques on page 59.
5. Position backing, batting, and quilt top. Pin, baste, quilt, and bind according to directions in Glossary of Techniques on pages 60-61.

This quilt could also be made by setting the blocks on the diagonal, thereby eliminating a few of the smaller pieces.

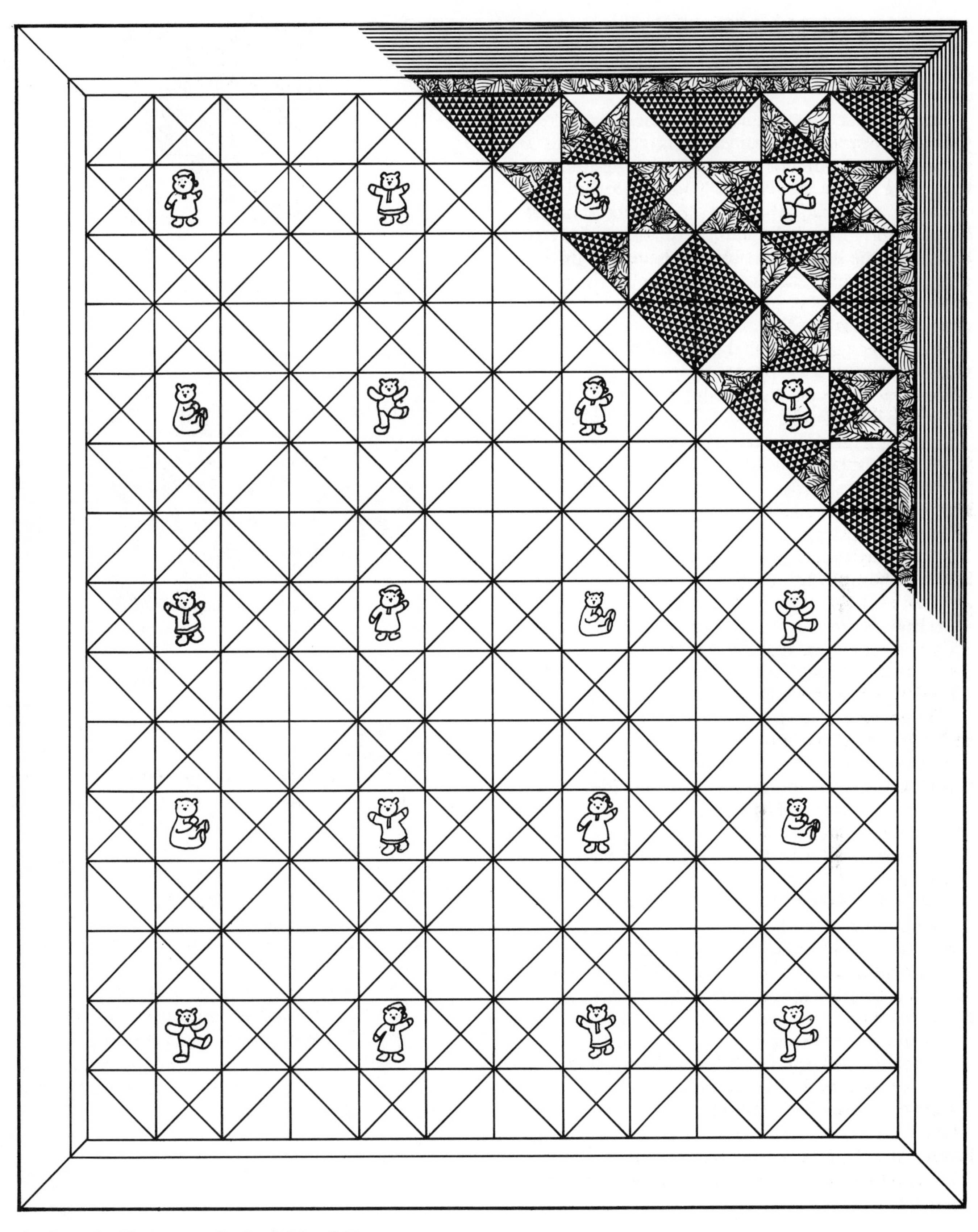

Anthony's Christmas Quilt, 54″ x 66″

Rainbow Trout

Color photo on page 29.

One of the secrets in this quilt is the eyes. Take a look at nice dress fabric and find a large polka dot or novelty print from which to cut the eye circles. You may have to look awhile, and be prepared for an interesting response when you announce you are looking for "fish eye" fabric. You may wish to reverse some of the fish blocks; just turn upside down before appliqueing on the eyes.

Size: 42″ x 50″

Materials: 45″ wide fabric
1/8 yd. each of 6 colors for fish back
2/3 yd. for fish front
1/8 yd. for eyes
1 1/4 yds. for background
1/3 yd. for first border
2/3 yd. for second border
1/2 yd. for binding
1 2/3 yds. for backing
45″ x 60″ baby quilt batting

Cutting: Strips are approximately 45″ long, cut from selvage to selvage.

From each of 6 prints for fish back:
- 2 strips, 1 1/2″ wide

From print for fish front:
- 2 strips, 8 7/8″ wide
  Subcut into 6 squares, 8 7/8″, then diagonally cut into 12 triangles.

From print for eyes:
- 12 Template A plus 1/4″ seam allowance
- 12 Template A from heavy paper

From background:
- 2 strips, 8 1/2″ wide
  Subcut to 6 squares, 8 1/2″ x 8 1/2″, for alternate block.
- 1 strip, 12 1/2″ wide
  Subcut to 3 squares, 12 1/2″ x 12 1/2″, and cut twice diagonally to make setting squares.
- 2 squares, 8 7/8″ x 8 7/8″, cut diagonally to make 4 corners

From first border print:
- 5 strips, 1 1/2″ wide

From second border print:
- 5 strips, 3 1/2″ wide

From binding print:
- Cut into 2 1/2″ bias strips.

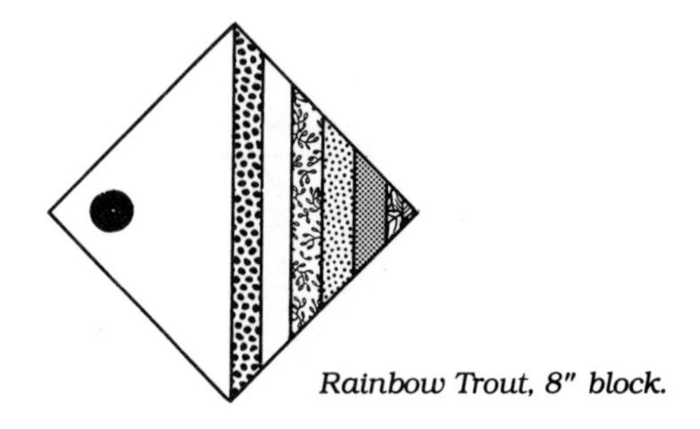

Rainbow Trout, 8″ block.

Sewing:

1. Sew 6 strips together for fish back in desired sequence on long sides. Repeat. Press seams in one direction. Make full-size Cutting Template B from cardboard. Carefully cut 6 from each piece, making 6 fish backs from each color sequence.

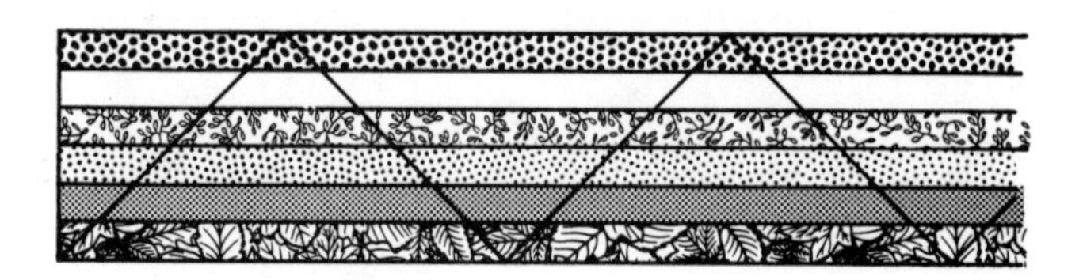

2. See paper-piecing directions in Glossary of Techniques on page 62 and applique eyes.
3. Join fish front to fish back.
4. Following quilt diagram on page 25, lay out, then sew fish blocks, setting squares, and corners in diagonal rows.
5. Sew short ends of first border strips together. Repeat for second border strips. Join long sides of these strips together to make 1 long strip. Press and sew borders to quilt top as described in Glossary of Techniques on page 59.
6. Position backing, batting, and top. Pin, baste, quilt, and bind according to directions in Glossary of Techniques on pages 60-61.

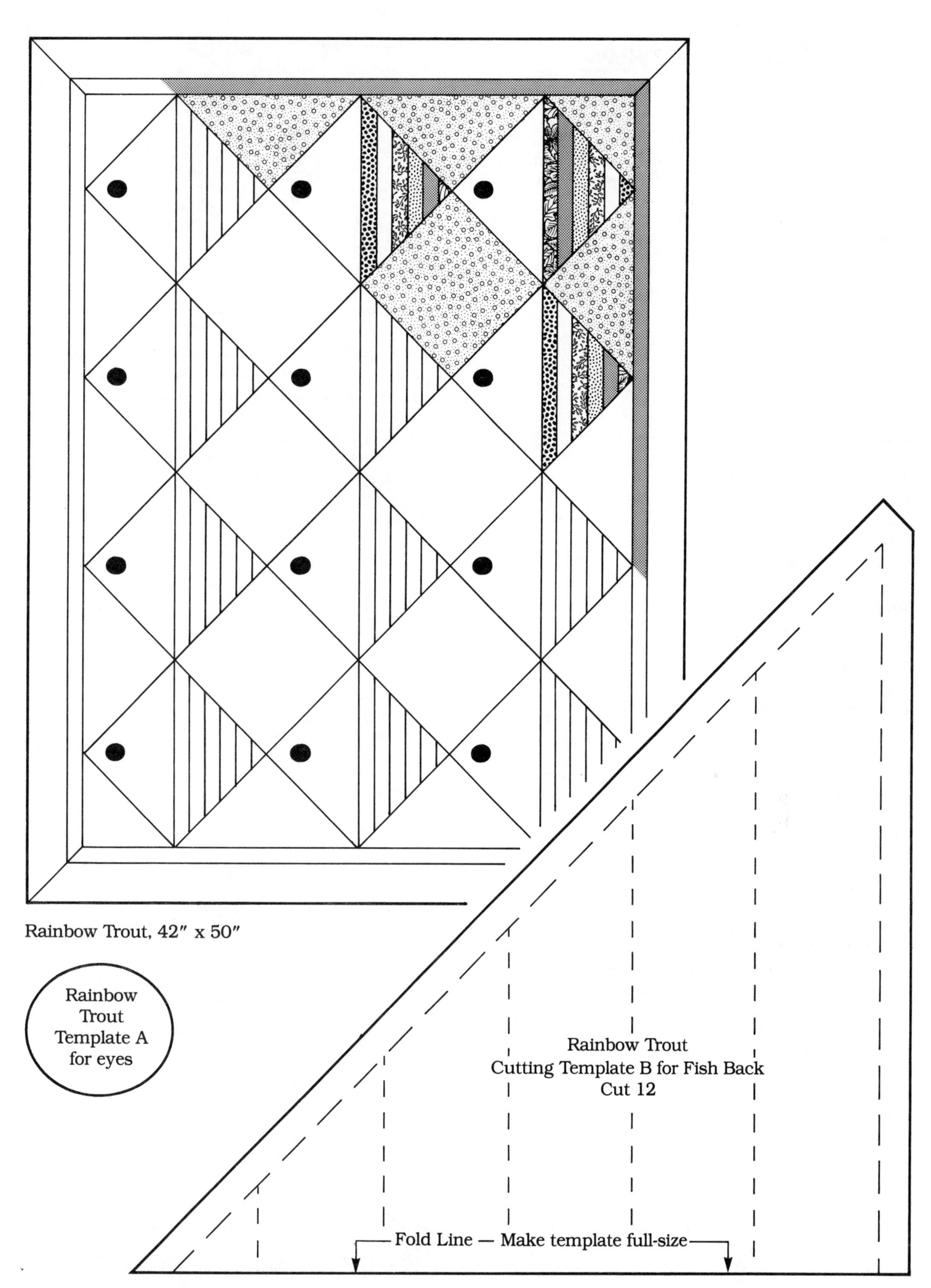

Rainbow Trout, 42″ x 50″

Froggy, Froggy

Color photo on page 29.

Here again you will want to look carefully for some special fabric for the frog eyes. Like the fish, be careful who overhears you muttering to yourself "just looking for frog eyes." Note that this is the voice of experience speaking!

Size: 40″ x 50″

Materials: 45″ wide fabric
1 1/2 yds. background and sashing
1 yd. green for frog body
2/3 yd. yellow for frog belly
1/4 yd. black for mouth
1/8 yd. for eyes
1/3 yd. yellow for bug bodies
1/8 yd. green for bug head
1/8 yd. stripe for bug legs
1/2 yd. for binding
1 1/2 yds. for backing
Permanent non-toxic pen or T-shirt paint
45″ x 60″ baby quilt batting

Cutting: Strips are approximately 45″ long, cut from selvage to selvage.

From background and sashing:
2 strips, 4 7/8″ wide, for frog
Subcut to 18 squares, 4 7/8″ x 4 7/8″, then cut diagonally to make 36 triangles.
4 strips, 2 1/2″ wide, for sashing
Subcut to 3 strips, 12 1/2″ wide, for vertical sashing.
2 strips, 26 1/2″ long, for horizontal sashing
2 strips, 32 1/2″ long, for top and bottom
2 strips, 3 1/2″ wide
Subcut to 2 strips, 40 1/2″ long for sides.
From background for bug border:
3 strips, 1 1/2″ wide
Subcut to 28 lengths of 4 1/2″.
3 strips, 1 7/8″ wide
Subcut to 56 squares, 1 7/8″ x 1 7/8″, then cut diagonally to make 112 triangles.
3 strips, 2″ wide
Subcut to 28 lengths of 2 1/2″.
3 strips, 1″ wide
Subcut to 28 lengths of 2 1/2″.
From green for frog:
3 strips, 4 7/8″ wide
Subcut to 18 squares, 4 7/8″ x 4 7/8″, then cut diagonally to make 36 triangles.
1 strip, 4 1/2″ wide
Subcut to 6 squares, 4 1/2″ x 4 1/2″.
1 strip, 5 1/4″ wide
Subcut to 3 squares, 5 1/4″ x 5 1/4″, then cut twice diagonally to make 12 triangles (3 extra).
From yellow for frog:
1 strip, 4 7/8″ wide

Frog block, 12″

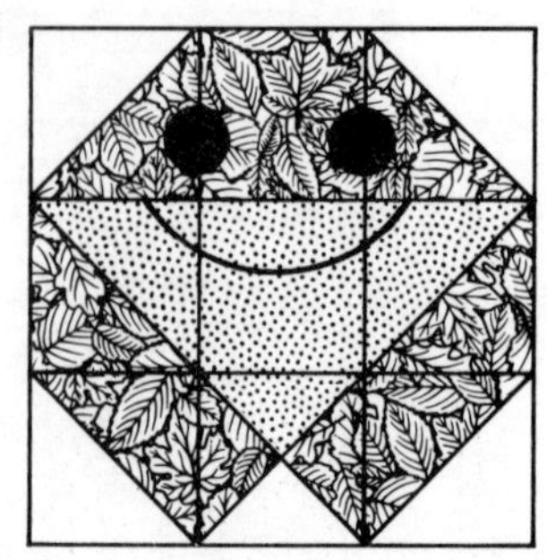

Subcut to 6 squares, 4 7/8″ x 4 7/8″, then cut diagonally to make 12 triangles.
1 strip, 4 1/2″ wide
Subcut to 6 squares, 4 1/2″ x 4 1/2″.
2 squares, 5 1/4″ x 5 1/4″, cut twice diagonally to make 8 triangles (2 extra)
From black:
6 bias strips, 3/4″ x 9″
From print for eyes:
12 Template A plus 1/4″ seam allowance
12 Template A from heavy paper
From yellow for bugs:
3 strips, 3 1/2″ wide
Subcut to 28 strips, each 4 1/2″ wide.
Using Cutting Template C in block corner, cut 2 corners on 1 long side.
From green for bug head:
3 strips, 2 1/2″ wide
Subcut to 28 squares, 2 1/2″ x 2 1/2″. Using Cutting Template C in block corner, cut 2 adjacent corners.
From stripe for legs:
3 strips, 1 1/2″ wide
Subcut to 28 units of 4 1/2″.

Sewing:

1. Following block piecing guide below, sew rows for 6 frog blocks. Do not stitch rows together.

Row 1

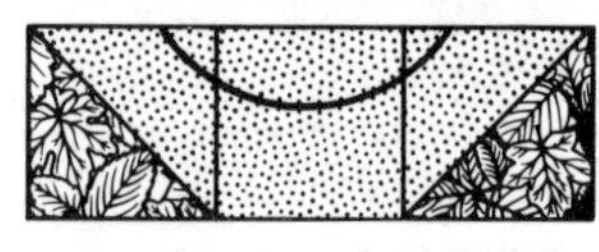

Row 2

Row 3

2. Using Mouth Template B and water erasable pen and keeping long template edge against edge of fabric, mark curved line for bias placement.

3. From bias strips for mouth, press long raw edge in 1/4″ toward center; repeat for other side. Applique to body, using marked line as a guide for inner curve.

4. Sew rows together making 6 frog blocks.

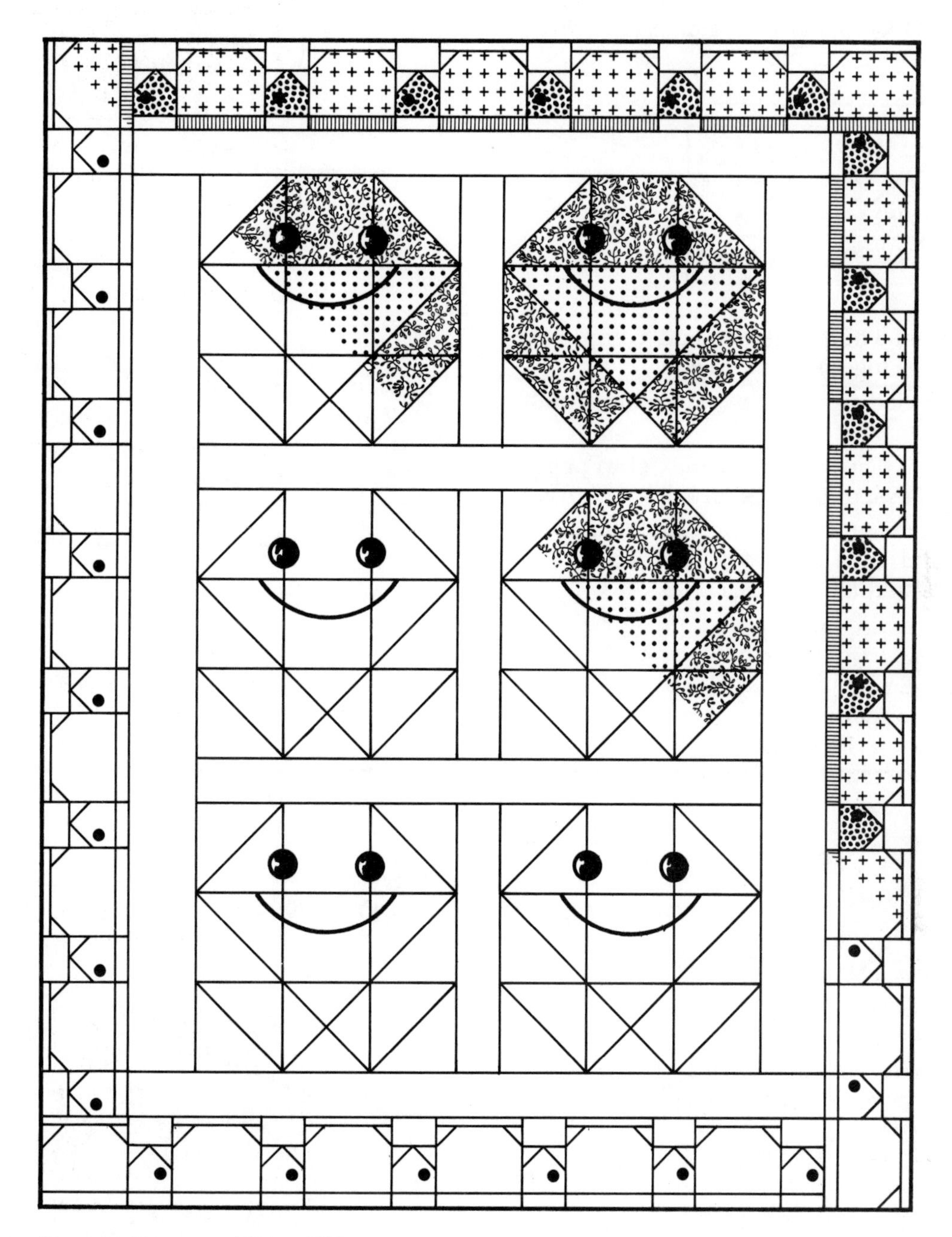

Froggy, Froggy, 40″ x 50″

5. Paper-piece and applique eyes according to directions in Glossary of Techniques on page 62.

6. Following quilt diagram on page 27, join blocks with sashing into 3 rows of 2 blocks. Join horizontal sashing to these rows, then add sides and top and bottom sashing.

7. Sew 28 bugs together following diagram below:

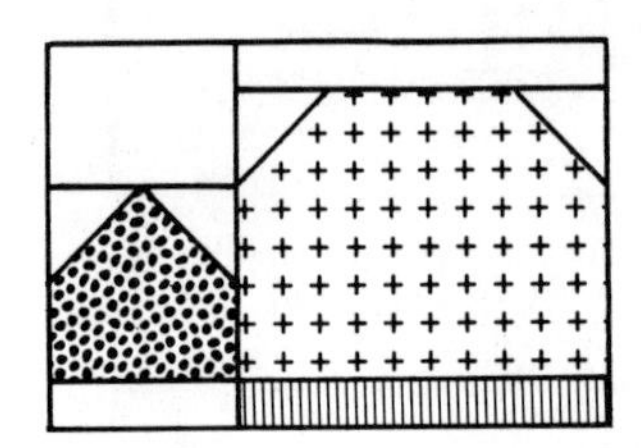

8. Sew 2 strips of 8 bugs together, end to end. Sew 2 strips of 6 bugs together, end to end.

9. Following quilt diagram on page 27, sew to quilt top.

10. Using non-toxic permanent pen, T-shirt paint, or embroidery floss, make eyes on bugs. Let dry.

11. Position backing, batting, and quilt top. Pin, baste, quilt, and bind according to directions in Glossary of Techniques on pages 60-61.

Froggy, Froggy
Cutting Template C
for Bug

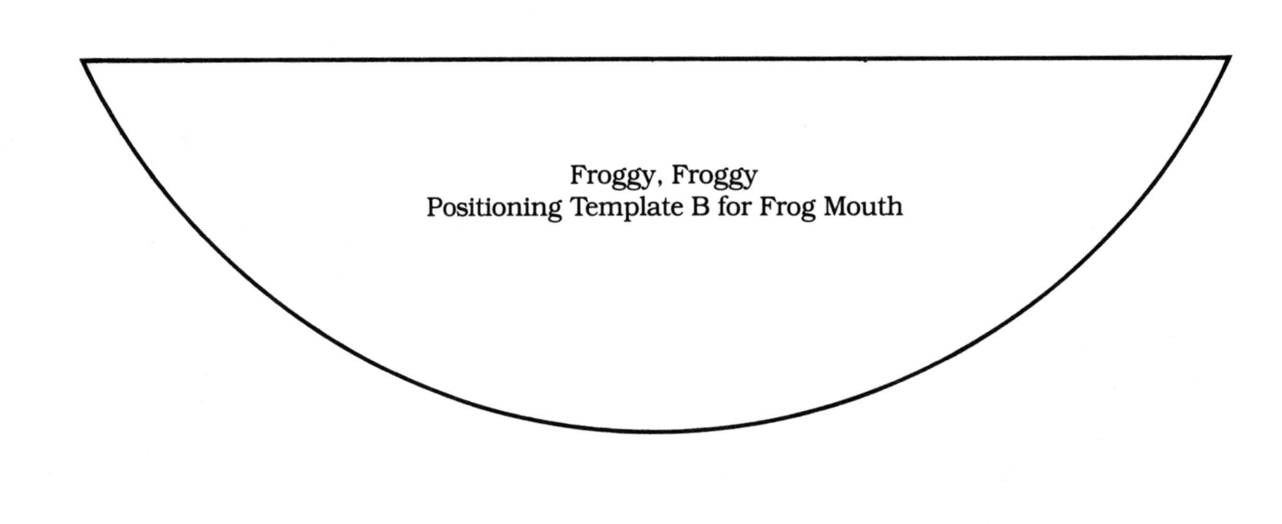

Left: It looks like Grandpa went fishing and caught "Rainbow Trout" (42″ x 50″). Look for interesting "water" fabric for this quilt. Owned and loved by Shane Eric Cote, who can hardly wait to go fishing with Grandpa.

Below: Happy frogs and bugs peer from behind the grass. Six frogs are surrounded by many 1000-legged worms. Happy-faced "Froggy, Froggy" (40″ x 50″) will make any child (or adult) chuckle.

Left: Even whales have to go to school. It looks like this quilt caught them practicing their spouting techniques—with need for improvement, judging by the quilting lines. A "school" of tiny fish swim around the whales. "Whales in School" is 45″ x 56″.

Right: Bright rainbow colors make this playroom a cheerful place. "Rainbow Kites" (42" x 52") remind one of blustery March days which are ideal for kite flying. Speed cutting and piecing techniques make these kites ready to fly in a few short hours.

Above: Careful arranging of colors in the Snowball block corners form a secondary pattern to make this "Snowball" quilt (42" x 53") a real zinger for bright baby eyes to watch.

Right: Remember your first day of school and the new box of crayons that you got, which had to last all year? Remember how carefully you set them in rows, then rearranged them several times to get them just right? "Box of Crayons" (42" x 56") recaptures this memory of childhood. Arrange the crayons by color, or randomly, for a delightful quilt. Try using pastel chintz or very dark colors for a unique look.

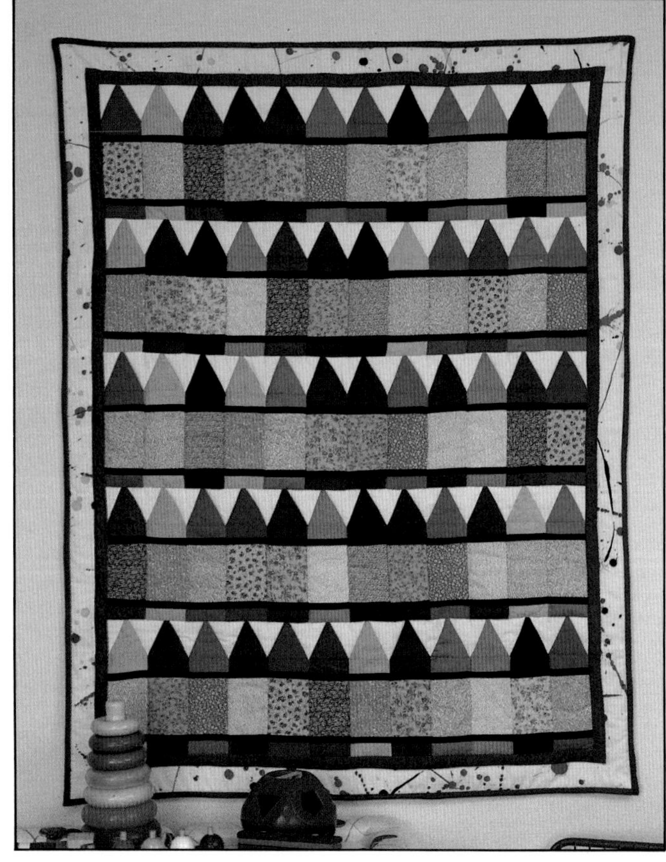

Above: Christmas quilts are special. Christmas quilts for grandchildren are extra special. Why not start a tradition of making one for each grandchild? "Anthony's Christmas Quilt" (54" x 66"), a variation of Ohio Star, is easy to make for a start. The preprinted bear fabric makes an interesting design. Owned and loved by Anthony Ryan Cote.

Right: When I was a child, the word "quilt" meant only one pattern. That pattern was the Nine-patch. The print squares were always in the corners, and the matching solid squares completed the design. The randomly placed squares in "Primary Nine-Patch" (42" x 50") look like jewels against the white background. Easy strip piecing and pieced sashing make this quilt a real gem.

Left: These bunnies appear to be content in this setting. They brought carrots for their "Bunny Lunch" (40″ x 54″). The bunnies are quickly assembled and have a delicate look when made of white overprinted muslin. The carrots take a little time to make, but are worth it. Bunny rocker from Heartland Interiors.

Below left: Careful fabric selection for the Nine-patch blocks will add another design element to this heart quilt. The ruffled eyelet border makes this quilt very feminine. Delight a baby or treat yourself to "Frilly Hearts" (36″ x 48″).

Below right: The traditional Double Irish Chain pattern turns into "Irish Bear Chain" (42″ x 58″) when a teddy bear is carefully quilted in the center of alternate blocks. They appear to be shy. Speed cutting and piecing techniques are used to bring this quilt to life.

Above: This humorous "Pussy Cats" quilt (42" x 56") is quickly pieced. Vary the eyes to have the cats look at or away from each other. Mice march around the edge of the quilt, looking for their cheese lunch. The cats are prowling too, looking at each other—or are they ready for an easy lunch too?

Left: This quilt is a combination of "Amish Mice" and "Cats" (40" x 52"). Can you see the mice hiding from the hungry eyes of the prowling cats? This quilt is a good example of the role that fabric choice plays in making a quilt. See pages 34 and 35 for other variations. Furniture from Heartland Interiors.

Left: This "Cats" quilt (40″ x 52″) really comes to life when made in primary colors. Easily assembled blocks are framed for emphasis. This must be a cat convention, and there are no mice in sight.

Below: The twist block has been around for a long time, and can be turned so many different ways. "Baby Twist" (44″ x 50″) will have baby eyes moving very quickly in all directions. The pattern uses just two shapes and blocks are easily assembled. This is a fine quilt on which to begin if you are new to quilting.

Right: "Amish Mice" (40″ x 50″) poke their heads out of their holes to see if the coast is clear to look for dinner. The bright colors add brilliance and jewelled tones to the quilt, giving it an added touch. The border is easily cut and pieced, like the mice it surrounds.

Below: "Baby Rail" (44″ x 50″) is the quickest and easiest quilt in this book. The three fabrics are cut in strips, sewn, recut and made into blocks. This quilt can be tied and placed on baby's bed in a few short hours, even if you are a beginner.

Right: Ducks swimming on the pond, with butterflies overhead, bring memories of warm summer days. The pieces in "Duckyflies" (42" x 56") are easy to work with and to handle. This quilt will be ready to give to eager small hands in a short period of time.

Below: These playful fish live in the old fishing hole, for now. They look hungry, but they'd better watch what they eat. Another quickly pieced and finished quilt for someone special, "Fishy, Fishy" (42" x 51") is made for fishermen of all ages.

Duckyflies

Color photo on page 36.

You may add eyes as you choose, depending on the print, or they may be omitted. This whimsical quilt will delight any youngster.

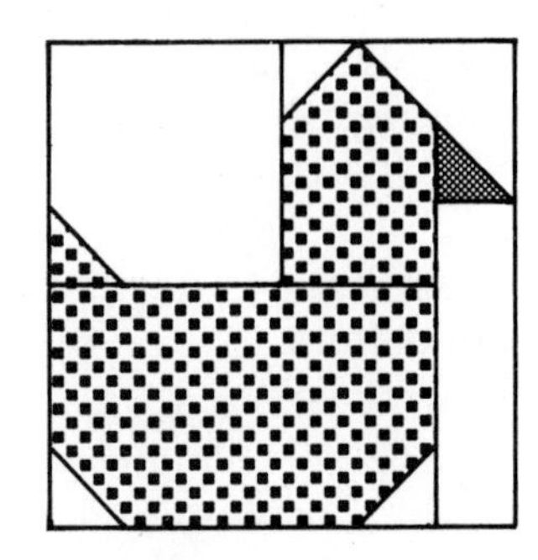

Duckyflies, 12″ block

Size: 42″ x 56″

Materials:
1/4 yd. each of 6 prints for ducks.
1 1/3 yds. background
1/2 yd. sashing
1/2 yd. first border
17 squares, 5 1/4″ x 5 1/4″, of prints for butterflies
1/2 yd. binding
1 2/3 yds. backing
45″ x 60 ″ baby quilt batting
Permanent non-toxic pen, T-shirt paint, or embroidery floss

Cutting: Strips are approximately 45″ long, cut from selvage to selvage.

From each of 6 prints for ducks:
A: 1 piece, 6 1/2″ x 10 1/2″. Using Cutting Template A in corners, cut 2 corners off 1 long side.
B: 1 piece 4 1/2″ x 6 1/2″. Using Cutting Template A in corners, cut 2 corners off 1 short side.
C: 1 square, 2 7/8″ x 2 7/8″, diagonally cut to make 2 triangles (1 extra)
From random duck prints for sashing corners:
4 squares, 2 1/2″ x 2 1/2″
From background:
C: 1 strip, 2 7/8″ wide
Subcut to 9 squares, 2 7/8″ x 2 7/8″, then cut diagonally to make 18 triangles.
D: 1 strip, 6 1/2″ wide
Subcut to 6 squares, 6 1/2″ x 6 1/2″. Place Cutting Template A in corner, cut off 1 corner.
E: 1 strip, 4 7/8″ wide
Subcut to 3 squares, 4 7/8″ x 4 7/8″, then cut diagonally to make 6 triangles.
F: 2 strips, 2 1/2″ wide
Subcut to 6 lengths of 8 1/2″ each.
4 squares, 4 1/2″, for border corners
3 strips, 5 1/4″ wide
Subcut to 17 squares, 5 1/4″ x 5 1/4″, then cut twice diagonally to make 68 triangles.
2 strips, 4 1/2″ wide
Subcut to 30 lengths of 1 1/2″ for butterfly sashing strips.
From beak fabric:
3 squares, 2 7/8″ x 2 7/8″, cut diagonally to make 6 triangles

From sashing:
5 strips, 2 1/2″ wide
Subcut to 3 lengths of 12 1/2″ for vertical sashing.
4 lengths of 26 1/2″ for horizontal sashing
2 lengths of 40 1/2″ for sides
From first border print:
3 strips, 2 1/2″ wide
Subcut to 2 lengths of 44 1/2″ for sides.
2 strips, 3″ wide
Subcut to 2 lengths of 30 1/2″ for top and bottom.
4 rectangles, 2 1/2″ x 3″
From prints for butterflies:
17 squares, 5 1/4″ x 5 1/4″, cut twice diagonally to make 68 triangles
From binding:
Cut into 2 1/2″ bias strips.

Sewing:
1. Following block piecing guide below, sew 6 duck blocks.

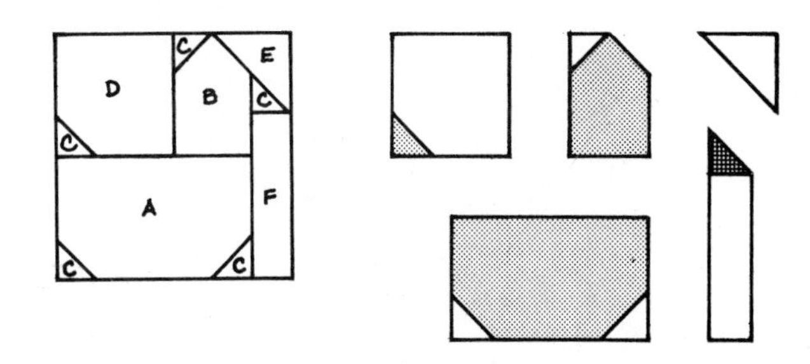

2. Following quilt diagram on page 39, sew sashing strips to blocks. Add first border, being careful to use 2 1/2″ strips on sides and 3″ strips on top and bottom.
3. Make 34 butterflies. Make 2 from each print.

4. Join 10 butterflies alternately with sashing strips. Repeat for second strip. Do the same with 7 units. Add 4 1/2″ corner squares to ends of shorter units.

5. Sew longer unit strips to sides, and shorter unit strips to top and bottom.

6. Using permanent non-toxic pen, T-shirt paint, or embroidery floss, add antennas and let dry.

7. Position backing, batting, and quilt top. Pin, baste, quilt, and bind according to directions in Glossary of Techniques on pages 60-61.

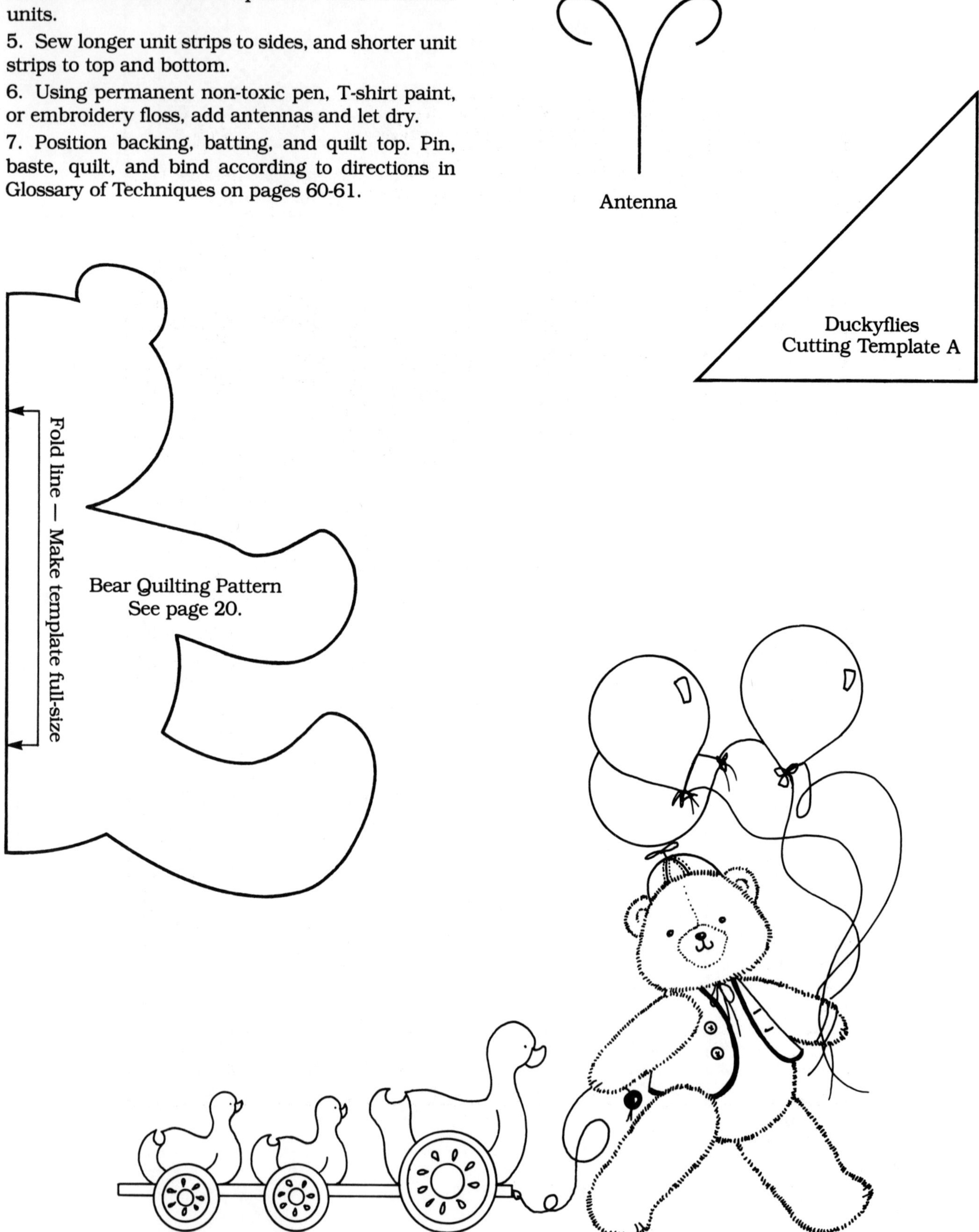

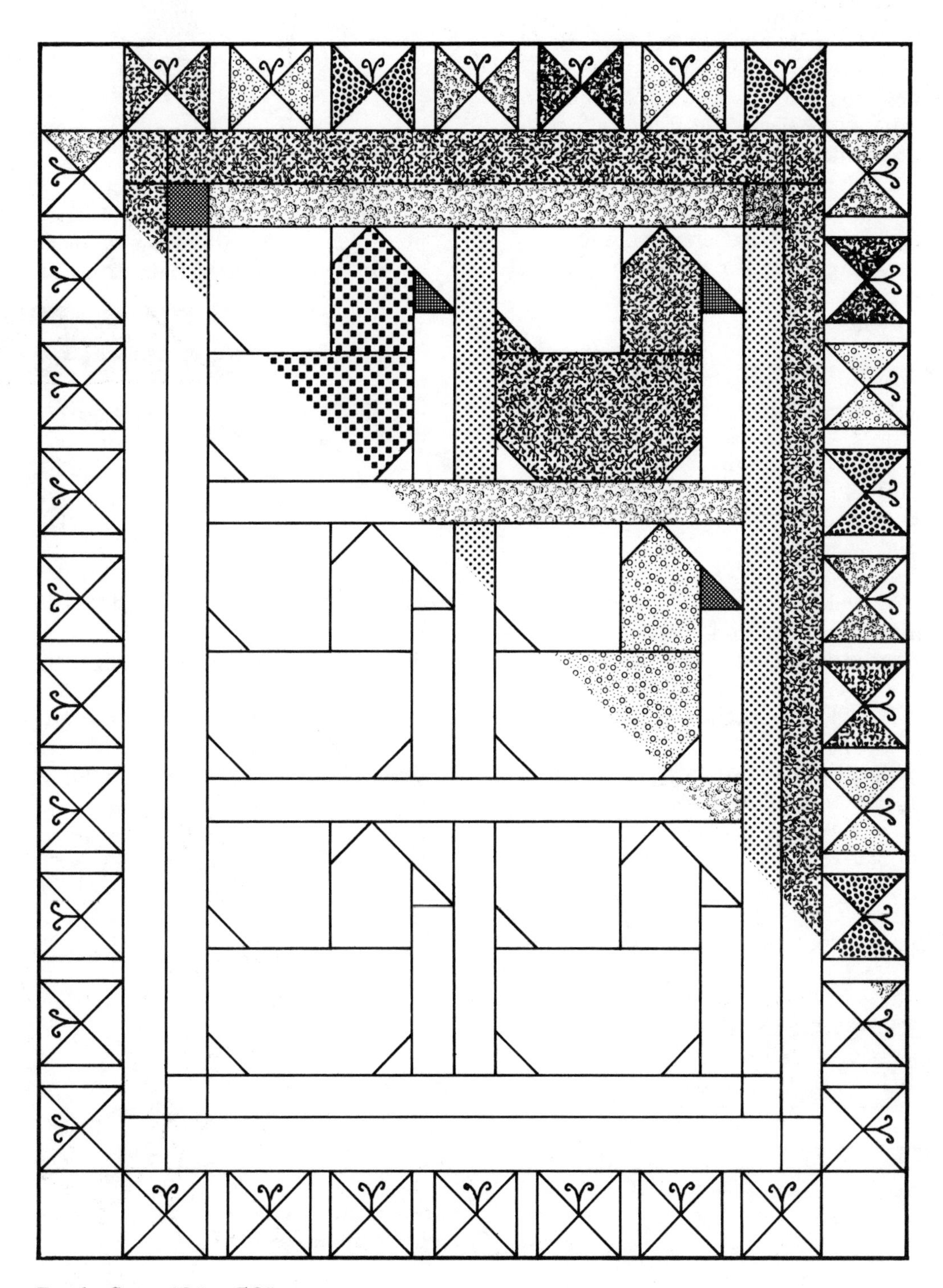

Duckyflies, 42″ x 56″

Rainbow Kites

Color photo on page 30.

Before sewing blocks into rows, experiment with alternate block placement. You can make a number of interesting, bold graphic designs in this quilt. Branch out and make this design truly yours.

Size: 42″ x 52″

Materials: 45″ wide fabric

3/8 yd. each of red, orange, yellow, green, blue, and purple for kites
3/4 yd. solid color for first border and binding
1 yd. print for background and second border
1 2/3 yds. for backing
45″ x 60″ baby quilt batting

Cutting: Strips are approximately 45″ long, cut from selvage to selvage.

From orange, yellow, green, and blue:
 7 strips, 1 1/2″ wide
From red and purple:
 7 strips, 1 3/4″ wide
From background:
 1 strip, 9 3/4″ wide
  Subcut into 4 squares, 9 3/4″ x 9 3/4″, then cut squares twice diagonally to make Setting Triangles.
 5 strips, 3 1/2″ wide, for second border
 2 squares, 7″ x 7″.
  Subcut diagonally for corners.
From first border and binding color:
 5 strips, 1 1/2″ wide
 Cut remaining 1/2 yd. into 2 1/2″ bias strips.

Sewing:

1. Sew 7 sets of colored strips lengthwise in this order:

Rainbow Kites, 6″ block

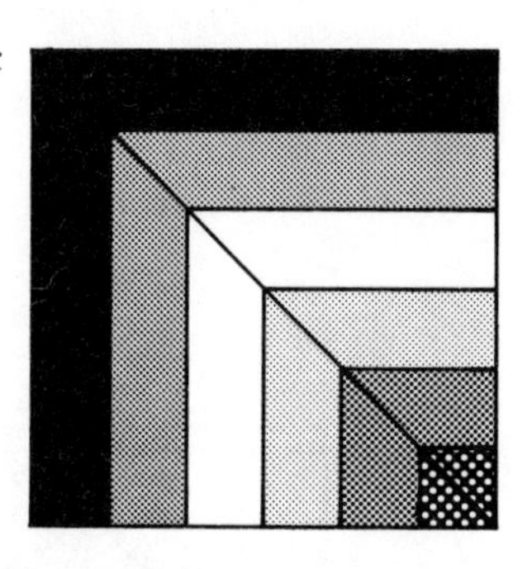

2. Position two sets of strips with right sides together, matching seams. Using Cutting Template A, cut in pairs following placement diagram below. You will get 10 pairs from each set.

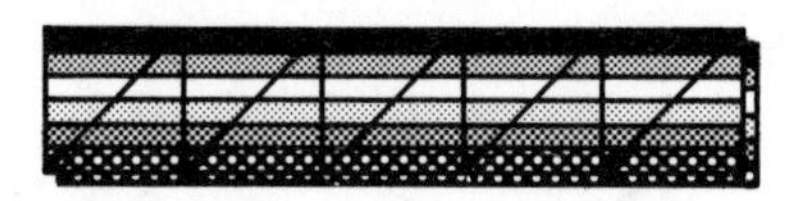

3. Match pairs and sew to make 20 Block A and 12 Block B. Trim blocks to 6 1/2″.

Block A

Block B

4. Following quilt diagram on page 41, arrange and sew rows diagonally with Setting Triangles for quilt top.

5. Sew 1 1/2″ strips for first border, on short sides, to make 1 long strip. Repeat for second border strips. Join long sides of these strips together to make 1 long strip. Press and sew borders to top as described in Glossary of Techniques on page 59.

6. Position backing, batting, and quilt top. Pin, baste, quilt, and bind according to directions in Glossary of Techniques on pages 60-61.

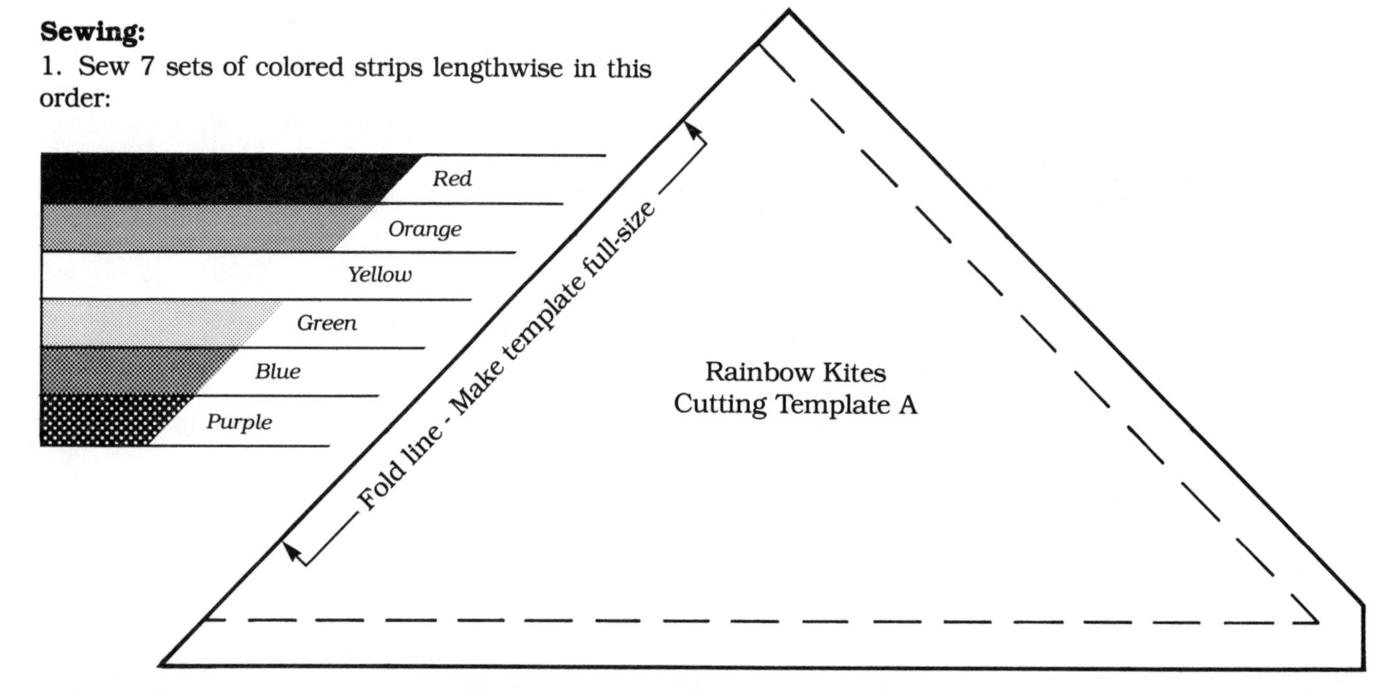

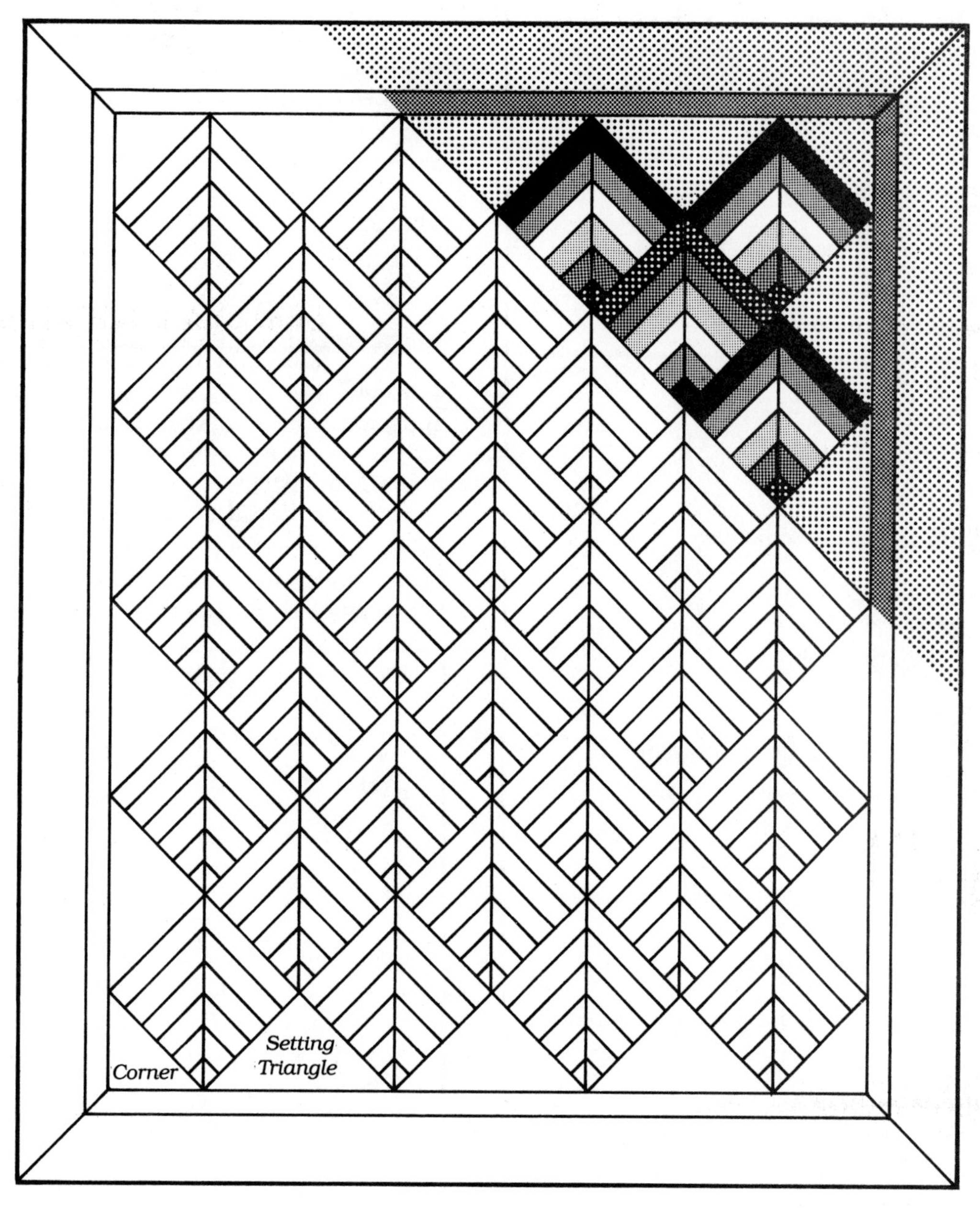

Rainbow Kites, 42″ x 52″

Box of Crayons

Color photo on page 30.

Different prints will give a different look to each quilt. For contrast, use light prints for crayon wrappers. For a set of deeper colors, use the darker prints. You may want to applique a broken top or torn wrapper on several crayons for a more realistic box of crayons.

Size: 42″ x 56″

Materials: 45″ wide fabric
1/4 yd. each of 12 prints
1/4 yd. each of 12 coordinating solid colors
2/3 yd. solid for first border and binding
1/2 yd. print for second border
3/8 yd. black solid
1/2 yd. background
1 2/3 yds. backing
45″ x 60″ baby quilt batting

Cutting: Strips are approximately 45″ long, cut from selvage to selvage.

From each of 12 prints:
1 strip, 4 1/2″ x 22″
From each coordinating solid:
1 strip, 1 1/2″ wide
1 strip, 3 1/2″ wide
Subcut into 5 triangles from Template A.
From black:
12 strips, 1″ wide
From background:
4 strips, 3 1/2″ wide
Subcut to 55 Template A and 5 Template B and 5 reversed Template B.
From first border and binding solid:
6 strips, 1 1/2″ wide
Cut remaining fabric into 2 1/2″ bias strips.
From second border print:
6 strips, 2 1/2″ wide

Sewing:

1. For each color crayon, sew strips together as shown below (black and solid color strips have been cut in half for 22″ lengths):

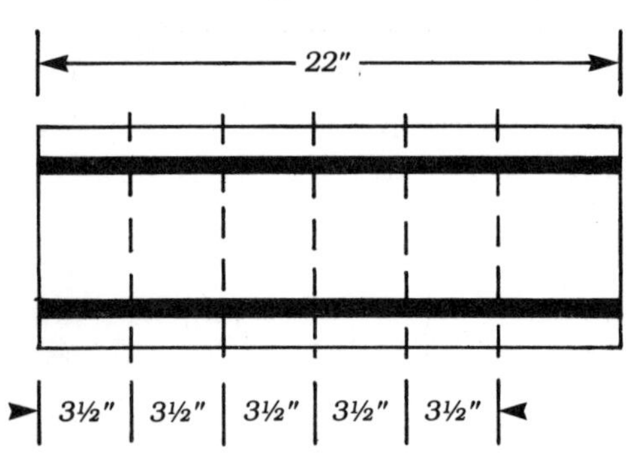

Subcut each sewn unit into 5 segments, each 3 1/2″ long.

2. Arrange into 5 rows of 12 each, varying the color order in each row. Lay out matching solid triangles and background triangles and sew together as in quilt diagram on page 43, being sure that colors match. Sew Template B pieces at each row end.

3. Before sewing rows together, blunt tips of crayons by cutting off the 1/4″ seam allowance on triangle rows so points of crayons are at raw edges (see diagram). Join rows together with 1/4″ seam, remembering that tips will be cut off.

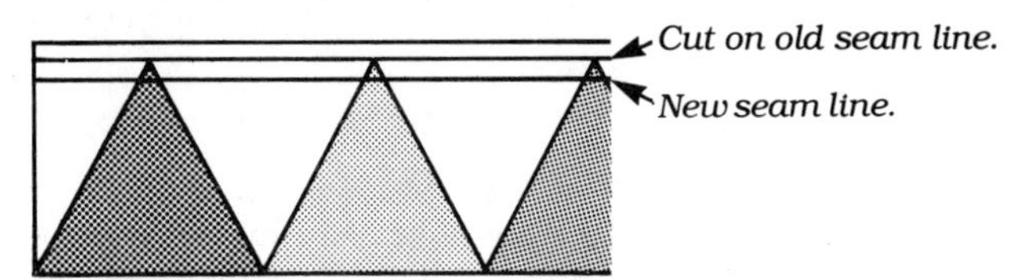

4. Sew 1 1/2″ first border strips together on short ends to make 1 long strip. Repeat for second border strips. Join long sides of these strips together to make 1 long strip. Press and sew borders to top as described in Glossary of Techniques on page 59.

5. Position backing, batting, and quilt top. Pin, baste, quilt, and bind according to directions in Glossary of Techniques on pages 60-61.

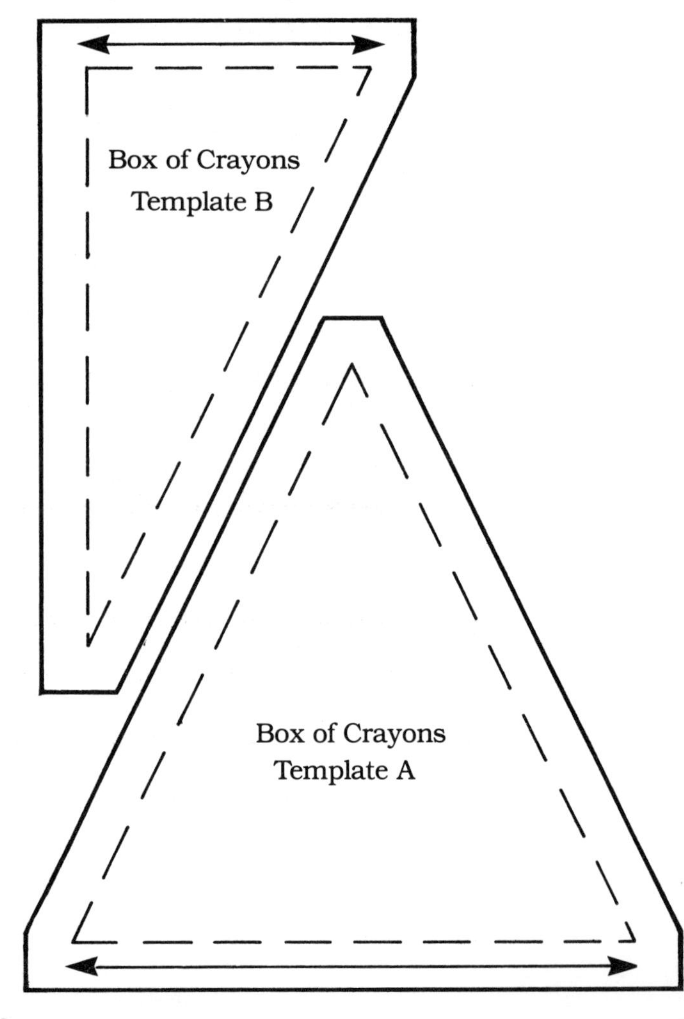

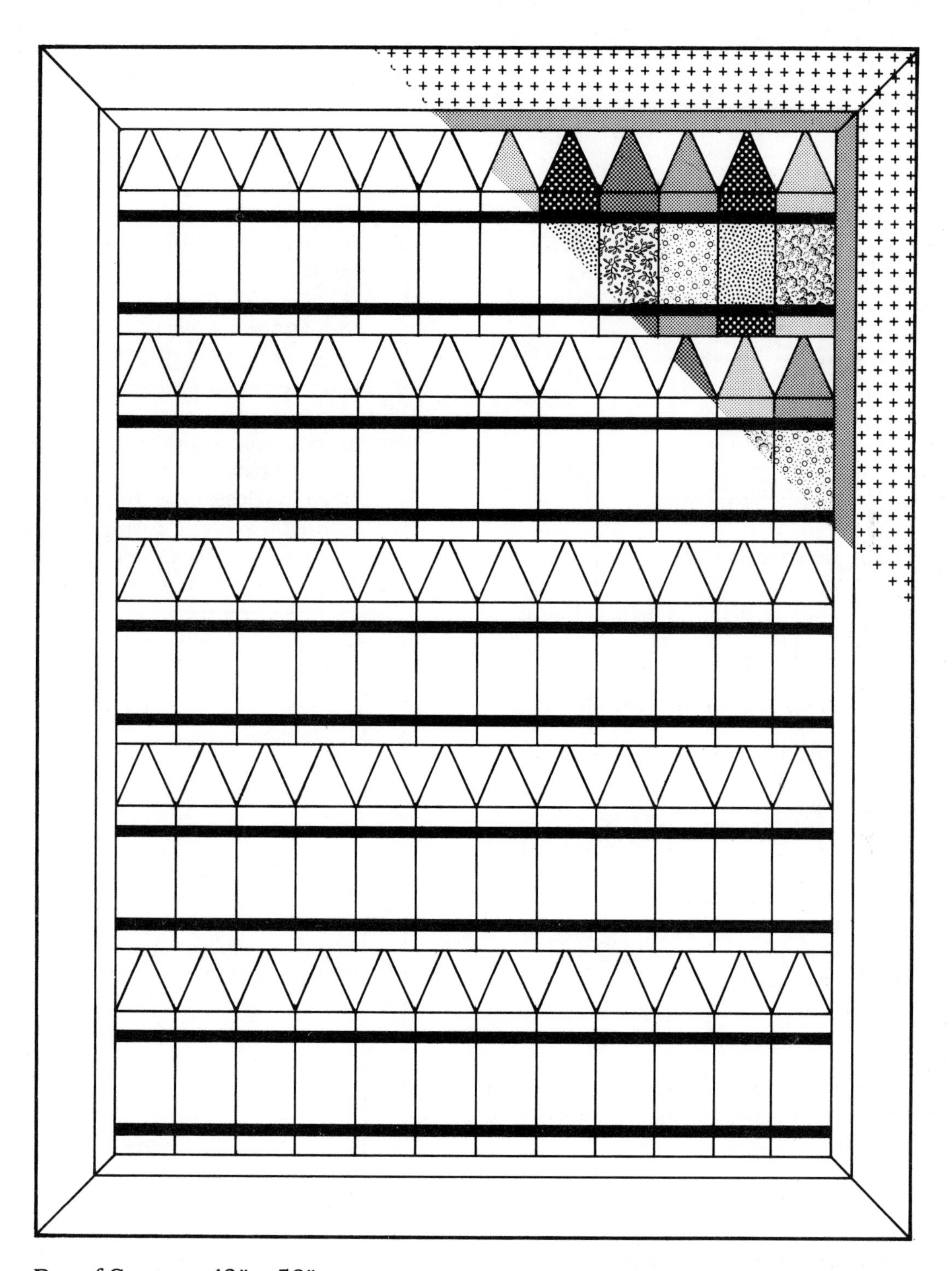

Box of Crayons, 42″ x 56″

Fishy, Fishy

Color photo on page 36.

Here is another design where you may use a novelty print for eyes. You can have fish swimming in either direction by turning the block upside down before sewing on eyes. See what fun you can have with block arrangement on this one! Kissing fish?

Size: 42″ x 51″

Materials: 45″ wide fabric
1/3 yd. each of 5 prints for fish
1/8 yd. print for eyes
2/3 yd. background
1/4 yd. for first border
3/8 yd. for second border
1 2/3 yds. for backing
1/2 yd. for binding
45″ x 60″ baby quilt batting

Cutting: Strips are approximately 45″ long, cut from selvage to selvage.

From each of 5 prints for fish body:
1 strip, 9 1/2″ wide
Subcut to 3 squares, 9 1/2″ x 9 1/2″. Using Cutting Template A, cut off 4 corners of each.
3 squares, 3 1/2″ x 3 1/2″
3 squares, 3 7/8″ x 3 7/8″, cut diagonally to make 6 triangles
From background print:
5 strips, 3 7/8″ wide
Subcut to 45 squares, 3 7/8″ x 3 7/8″, cut diagonally to make 90 triangles.
2 strips, 2″ wide
Subcut into 15 lengths, each 4″, for mouth.
From print for eyes:
Cut 15 Template B plus 1/4″ seam allowance.
Cut 15 Template B from heavy paper.
From first border print:
5 strips, 1 1/2″ wide
From second border print:
5 strips, 2 1/2″ wide
From binding:
Cut into 2 1/2″ bias strips.

Sewing:
1. Sew blocks together, following block piecing guide.

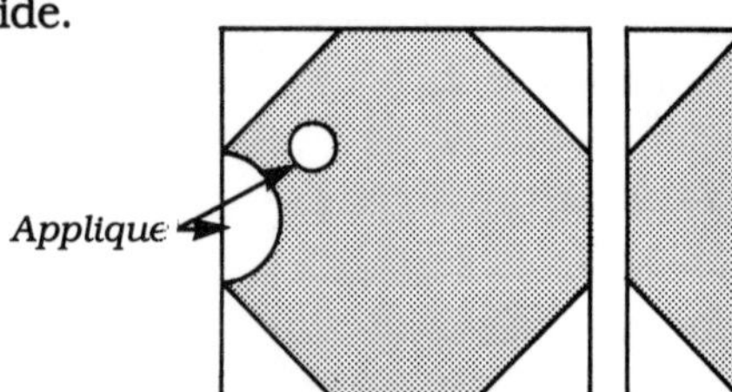

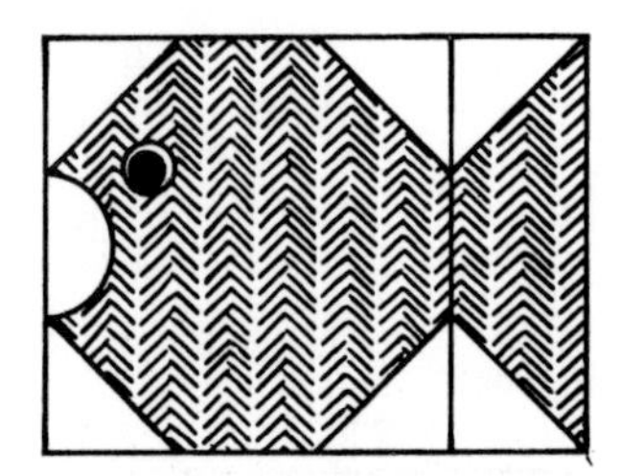

Fish, 9″ x 12″ block

2. Cut 15 of Mouth Template C from paper, then 15 plus 1/4″ seam allowance from 2″ background strip. Paper-piece and applique according to directions in Glossary of Techniques on page 62. Repeat for eyes using Eye Template B.
3. Following quilt diagram on page 45, join blocks into rows and sew rows together for quilt top.
4. Sew short ends of first border strips together. Repeat for second border strips. Join long sides of these strips together to make 1 long strip. Press and sew borders to top as described in Glossary of Techniques on page 59.
5. Position backing, batting, and top. Pin, baste, quilt, and bind according to directions in Glossary of Techniques on pages 60-61.

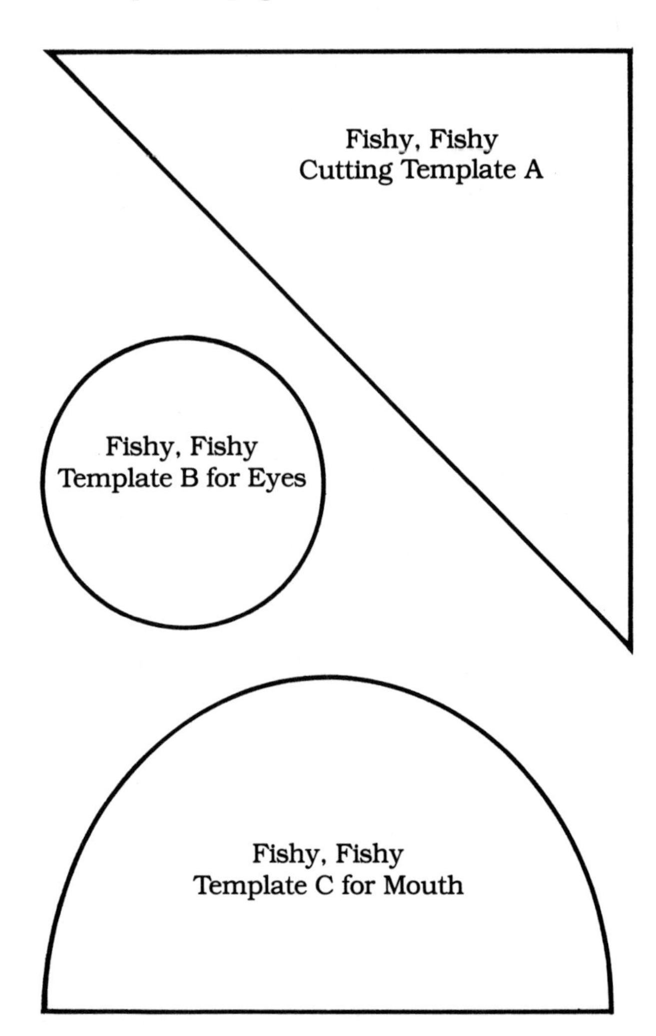

Fishy, Fishy, 42″ x 51″

Cats

Color photo on page 34.

This pattern can be interchanged with the Amish Mice in any way you desire. (See photo on page 32.) An interesting quilt can be made using both cats and mice. The background for the cats can "disappear" like the Amish Mice by making the block background, sashing, and setting triangles of the same fabric. The mice may also be framed like the cats. Perhaps you will want to hide some mice from the prowling cats. You can have a lot of fun with this design and the following two.

Size: 40″ x 52″

Materials: 45″ wide fabric
1/2 yd. block background
1 yd. for setting squares and second border
18 squares, each 8″ x 8″, for each cat
1/8 yd. for eyes
1/4 yd. for sashing on 6 blocks
1 1/4 yds. for sashing on 12 blocks, first border, and binding
1 1/2 yds. for backing
45″ x 60″ baby quilt batting
Permanent non-toxic pen or T-shirt paint

Cutting: Strips are approximately 45″ long, cut from selvage to selvage.

From block background:
For A: 1 strip, 3 3/8″ wide
Subcut to 18 pieces, 2 1/16″ long.
For D: 3 strips, 2 7/8″ wide
Subcut to 36 squares, 2 7/8″ x 2 7/8″, then cut diagonally to make 72 triangles.
From each cat print:
For B: 1 square, 3 11/16″ x 3 11/16″, cut diagonally to make 2 triangles
For C: 1 square, 2 1/4″ x 2 1/4″, cut diagonally to make 2 triangles
For D: 1 square, 2 7/8″ x 2 7/8″, cut diagonally to make 2 triangles
For E: 2 squares, 1 1/2″ x 1 1/2″
For F: 2 squares, 2 1/2″ x 2 1/2″
From eye print:
2 strips, 1 1/2″ wide
Subcut to 24 squares, 1 1/2″ x 1 1/2″
From sashing for 6 inner blocks:
5 strips, 1 1/2″ wide
Subcut to 12 pieces, each 6 1/2″ long, and 12 pieces, each 8 1/2″ long.
From sashing for 12 blocks:
11 strips, 1 1/2″ wide
Subcut to 24 pieces, each 6 1/2″ long, and 24 pieces, each 8 1/2″ long.
5 strips, 1 1/2″ wide, for first border

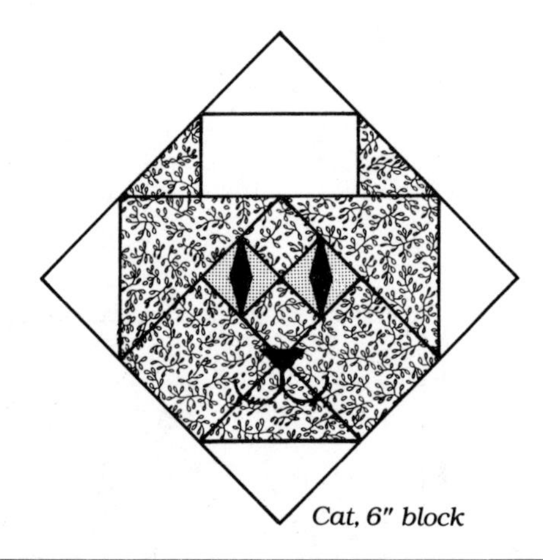
Cat, 6″ block

Cut 1/2 yd. into 2 1/2″ bias strips for binding.
From print for setting triangles:
3 squares, 12 3/4″ x 12 3/4″, cut twice diagonally to make 12 triangles
2 squares, 9″ x 9″, cut diagonally to make 4 triangles
5 strips, 2 1/2″ wide, for second border

Sewing:
1. Following block piecing guide, sew 18 blocks together. Square up blocks to 6 1/2″.

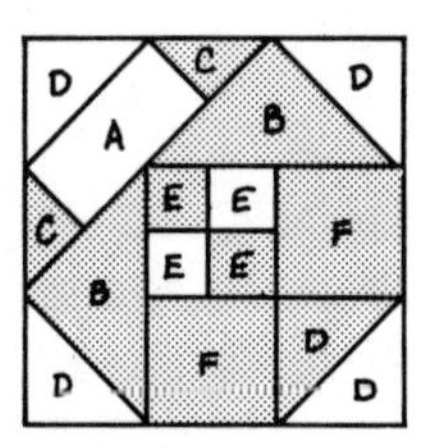

2. With permanent, non-toxic pen or embroidery floss, paint or sew on facial features shown below. Let dry.
3. Add sashing strips by sewing 6 1/2″ strips to opposite sides. Repeat for 8 1/2″ strips. Note that 12 blocks (top, bottom, and longer rows) have 1 color sashing and 6 inner blocks have another color.
4. Arrange blocks and setting triangles in diagonal rows. Sew in rows, then sew rows together for quilt top, following quilt diagram on page 47.
5. Sew short ends of first border strips together. Repeat for second border strips. Join long sides of these strips together to make 1 long strip. Press and sew borders to top as described in Glossary of Techniques on page 59.
6. Position backing, batting, and quilt top. Pin, baste, quilt, and bind according to directions in Glossary of Techniques on pages 60-61.

Facial features:

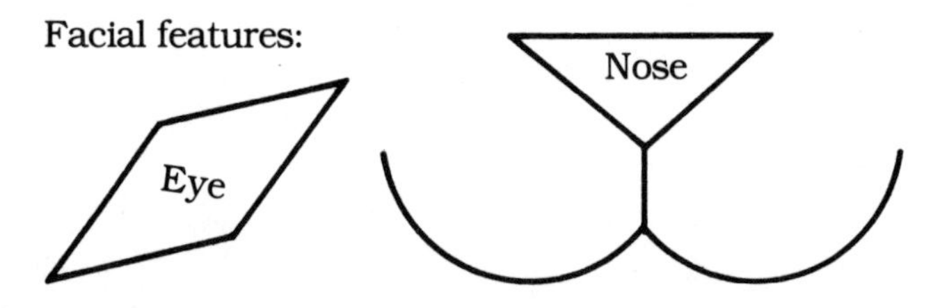

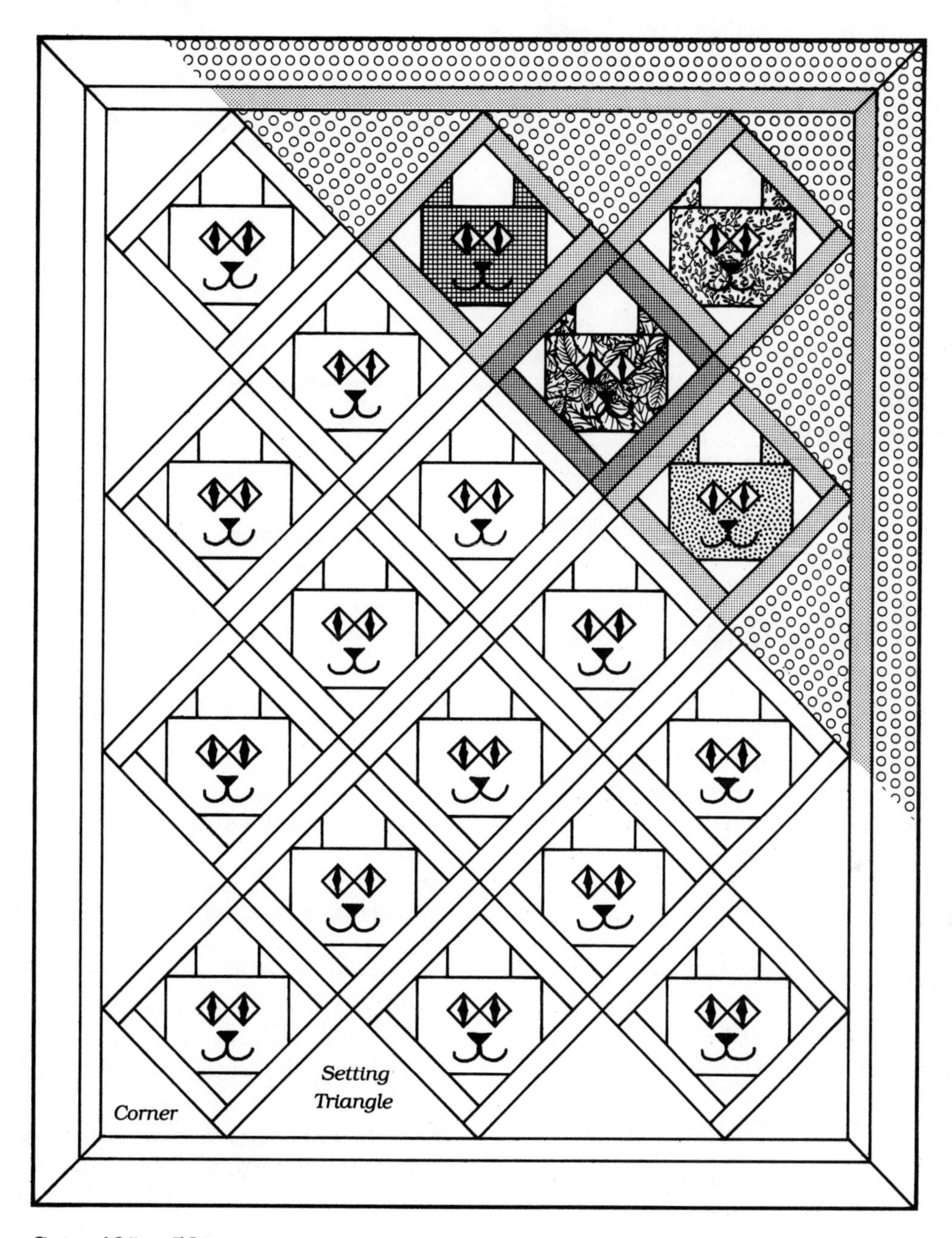

Cats, 40″ x 52″

Amish Mice

Color photo on page 35.

You may choose to use a contrasting color for pattern piece D or paint the eyes by hand, using the Mice Eyes template. Be sure to use a fabric that is light enough to show the painted lines. This design would also look well in bright calicoes. It's your turn to be the artist!

Size: 40″ x 52″

Materials: 45″ wide fabric
1 2/3 yds. background, sashing, setting, and corner squares
1/4 yd. for each mouse and border
1/8 yd. for noses
1/8 yd. for eyes
1/2 yd. for binding
1 1/2 yds. for backing
45″ x 60″ baby quilt batting
Permanent non-toxic pen or T-shirt paint

Cutting: Strips are approximately 45″ long, cut from selvage to selvage.

From background:
- 16 strips, 1 1/2″ wide, for sashing
  - Subcut to 36 segments, 6 1/2″ wide, and 36 segments, 8 1/2″ wide.
- 1 square, 3 1/2″ x 3 1/2″, for A
- 2 squares, 1 7/8″ x 1 7/8″, cut diagonally for C
- 4 squares, 3 1/2″ x 3 1/2″, for border corners
- 3 squares, 12 3/4″ x 12 3/4″, cut twice diagonally for 10 setting square triangles
- 2 squares, 9″ x 9″, cut diagonally for 4 corners

For each mouse:
- 1 strip, 1 1/2″ wide, for border
- 2 squares, 3 1/2″ x 3 1/2″, for B
- Using Cutting Template A, cut off 2 adjoining corners on each piece.
- 2 squares, 1 1/2″ x 1 1/2″, for D
- 2 pieces, 1 1/2″ x 2 1/2″, for E
- 1 square, 1 7/8″ x 1 7/8″, cut diagonally for C

For noses:
- 9 squares, 1 7/8″ x 1 7/8″, cut diagonally for C

For eyes:
- 36 squares, 1 1/2″ x 1 1/2″, for D

For binding:
Cut 1/2 yd. into 2 1/2″ bias strips.

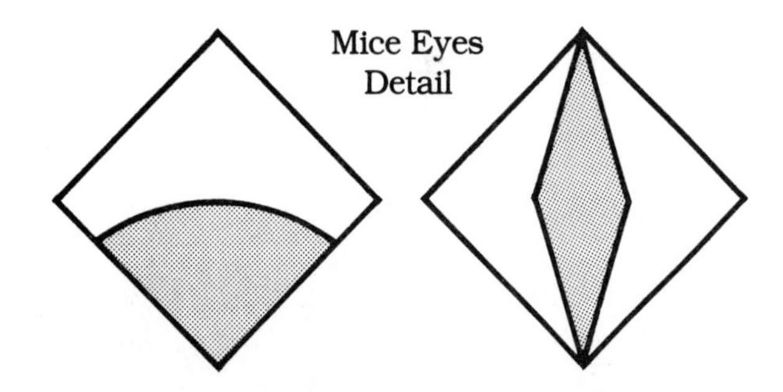

Mice Eyes Detail

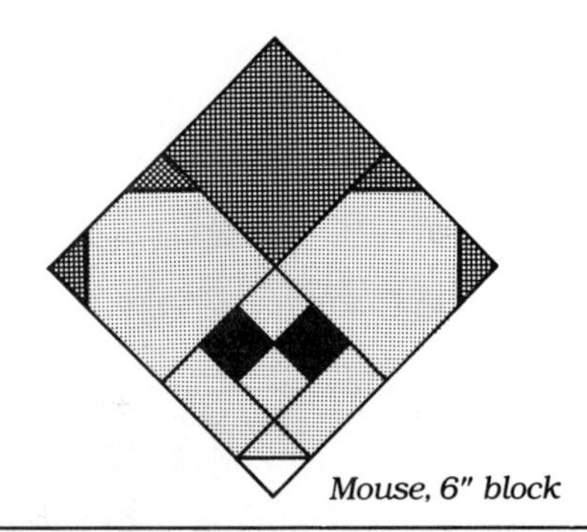

Mouse, 6″ block

Sewing:

1. Following block piecing guide, sew 18 blocks together. Square up blocks to 6 1/2″. Add detail to Mice Eyes (shown below) using non-toxic pen, paint, or embroidery floss.

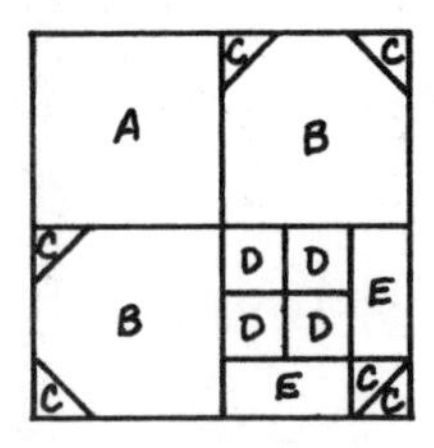

2. Add sashing by sewing 6 1/2″ strips to opposite sides. Repeat for 8 1/2″ strips.
3. Arrange blocks and setting triangles in diagonal rows. Sew in rows, then sew rows together for quilt top following quilt diagram on page 49.
4. Make pieced border. Cut a 1 1/2″ strip from each mouse fabric in half lengthwise. Randomly sew together on long sides in 2 sets of 18 colors.

   Subcut these 2 sets into 10 segments, each 3 1/2″ wide. Sew two 34-strip units and two 44-strip units.

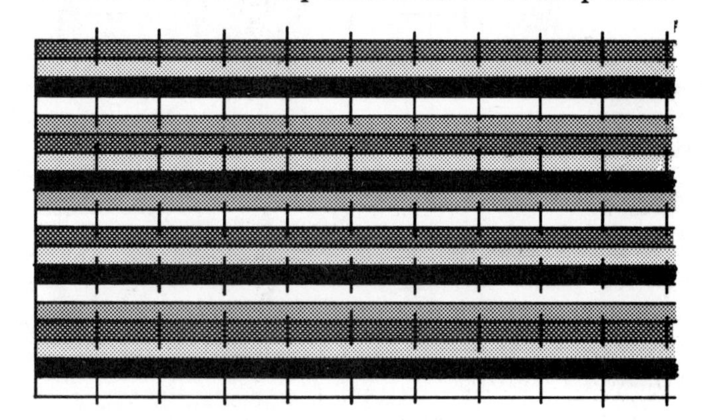

Sew 1 square, 3 1/2″ x 3 1/2″, to each end of shorter strips. Sew longer strip to each side and shorter strip to top and bottom.

5. Position backing, batting, and quilt top. Pin, baste, quilt, and bind according to directions in Glossary of Techniques on page 60-61.

Amish Mice
Cutting Template A:

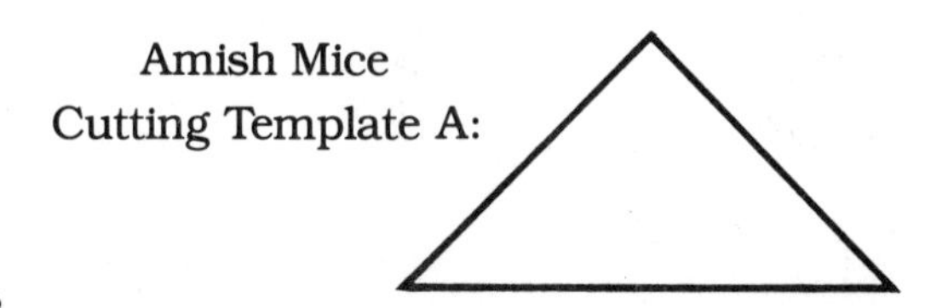

Amish Mice, 40″ x 52″

Pussy Cats

Color photo on page 33.

One fun thing about this quilt is that you can vary the cat eyes to look different ways: sideways at each other, up and down, or however you wish. You may wish to set the mice at a different angle. You may also reverse the cat by putting the tail on the right side and adjusting several of the body pieces. See what humor you can bring to this quilt.

Size: 42″ x 56″

Materials: 45″ wide fabric
1 yd. background
1/4 yd. of 6 prints for cats
3/8 yd. print for second border
1/8 yd. green for eyes
1/8 yd. black for eyes
1/2 yd. for sashing
5″ x 7″ yellow for cheese
19 squares, 5″ x 5″, of gray fabric for mice
1 2/3 yds. for backing
1/2 yd. for binding
45″ x 60″ baby quilt batting
Permanent non-toxic pen or T-shirt paint for detail marking

Cutting: Strips are approximately 45″ long, cut from selvage to selvage.

From background:
- 4 strips, 2 1/2″ wide
  - Subcut into 12 squares, 2 1/2″ x 2 1/2″, for B.
  - Subcut 6 pieces, 4 1/2″ x 2 1/2″ long, for G
- 6 Template D
- 6 and 6R Template F
- 6 squares, 2 7/8″ x 2 7/8″, cut diagonally for E
- 1 piece, 5″ x 7″
- 3 strips, 5″ wide
  - Subcut into 19 squares, 5″ x 5″.

From each cat fabric:
- 2 strips, 2 1/2″ wide
  - Subcut into 3 squares, 2 1/2″ x 2 1/2″, for B.
  - Subcut 3 pieces, 6 1/2″ x 2 1/2″ long, for C
  - Subcut 1 piece, 4 1/2″ x 2 1/2″ long, for G
  - Subcut 1 piece, 12 1/2″ x 2 1/2″ long, for H
- 2 Template D
- 6 squares, 2 7/8″ x 2 7/8″, cut diagonally for E

From green and black:
- 1 strip, each 1 1/2″ wide for A

From sashing:
- 7 strips, 2 1/2″ wide
  - Subcut into 3 pieces, each 12 1/2″ long.
  - Subcut 2 pieces, 26 1/2″ long
  - Subcut 2 pieces, 40 1/2″ long
  - Subcut 2 pieces, 30 1/2″ long

From gray fabric: 19 squares, 5″ x 5″
From yellow: 1 piece, 5″ x 7″
From border print: 6 strips, 2 1/2″ wide

Sewing:

1. Sew green and black pieces on long side. Press and cut into 12 segments, each 2 1/2″ long.
2. Lay out each cat and sew together according to diagram.

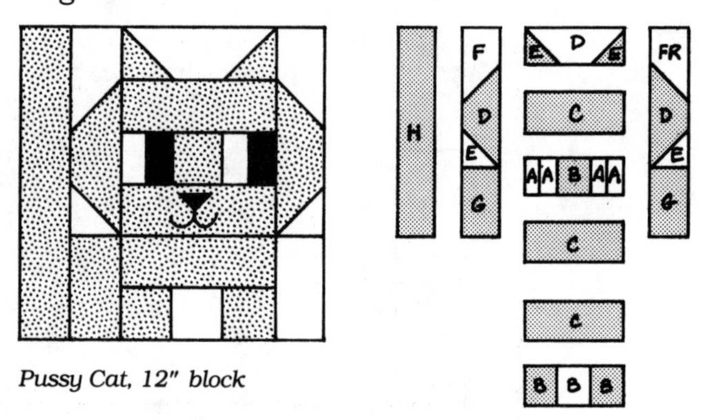

Pussy Cat, 12″ block

3. Join 2 blocks in 3 horizontal rows with 12 1/2″ sashing. Join these 3 rows with 26 1/2″ sashing pieces following quilt diagram on page 51. Add 40 1/2″ pieces to sides and 30 1/2″ pieces to top and bottom.
4. Make 38 mice:

With pencil, mark a diagonal line from corner to corner on the back of each 5″ background square. With right sides together, lay background square over each gray square and carefully stitch 1/4″ on each side of line. Cut on pencil line. Press open and square up to make a 4 1/2″ square.

5. For cheese, place 5″ x 7″ pieces of yellow and background right sides up. Mark diagonal line from corner to corner, as for mice, except this is a rectangle. Cut on diagonal line. Sew in 1/4″ seams to make rectangle. Press and square up to make 2 pieces, 4 1/2″ x 6 1/2″.
6. Using a permanent non-toxic pen, T-shirt paint, or embroidery floss, make cat face, mice eyes and tails, and cheese holes. Have 19 mice face to the left and 19 face to the right.
7. Following quilt diagram on page 51, join mice and cheese for border and sew to top.
8. Sew short ends of border strips together to make 1 long strip. Sew border to top as described in Glossary of Techniques on page 59.
9. Position backing, batting, and top. Pin, baste, quilt, and bind according to directions in Glossary of Techniques on pages 60-61.

Cat face detail

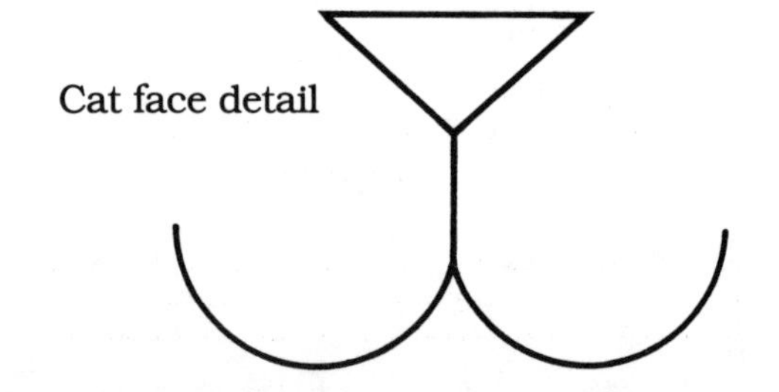

Pussy Cats, 42″ x 56″

Note: Smaller pieces overlap larger pieces, so be sure to include the entire template, including the space covered by the smaller piece, when you make the larger template.

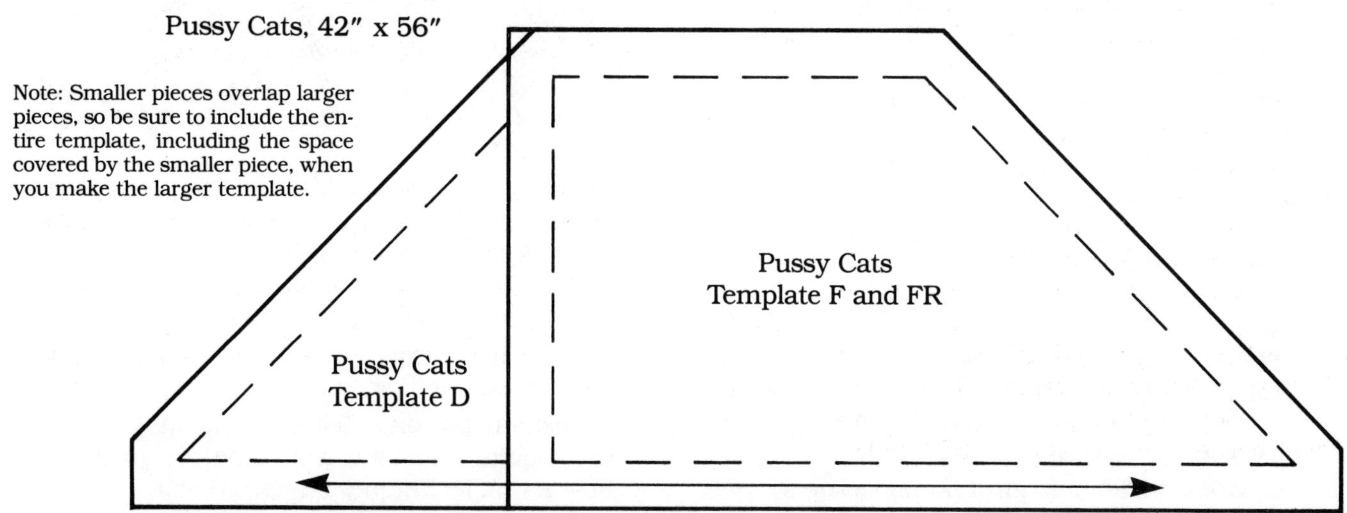

Bunny Lunch

Color photo on page 32.

This quilt looks very nice when you use the white overprinted muslin for the rabbits. The green background is lush, and, of course, with an ever-ready lunch all around, what bunny can complain?

You may wish to make the background and sashing all the same fabric, like the whale. This way, the bunnies appear to be sitting in the meadow, just waiting for lunch.

The bunny has the same configuration as the whale, so use the block piecing guide on page 54 and the templates on page 66, substituting appropriate colors.

Size: 40″ x 54″

Materials: 45″ wide fabric
1/4 yd. each of 6 prints for rabbits
2/3 yd. background
1/2 yd. sashing
1/3 yd. print for carrots
1/4 yd. print for carrot tops
2/3 yd. border background
Scrap for eyes
1/2 yd. for binding
1 2/3 yds. for backing
45″ x 60″ baby quilt batting

Cutting:
From each print for rabbit:
A: 1 square, 8 1/2″ x 8 1/2″. Use Cutting Template A in 2 opposite corners, and Cutting Template B in 1 corner.
B: 1 piece, 12 1/2″ x 4 1/2″. Use Cutting Template B in 2 corners on 1 long side.
E: 1 square, 2 7/8″ x 2 7/8″, cut diagonally to make 2 triangles (1 extra)
From background:
C: 2 strips, 4 7/8″ wide
Subcut to 9 squares, 4 7/8″ x 4 7/8″, then cut diagonally to make 18 triangles.
D: 1 strip, 2 1/2″ wide
Subcut to 6 squares, 2 1/2″ x 2 1/2″.
E: 1 strip, 2 7/8″ wide
Subcut to 9 squares, 2 7/8″ x 2 7/8″, then cut diagonally to make 18 triangles.
F: 1 strip, 4 1/2″ wide
Subcut to 6 lengths of 6 1/2″.
From scrap for eyes:
6 Template C plus 1/4″ seam allowance
6 Template C from heavy paper
From sashing:
6 strips, 2 1/2″ wide
Subcut to 2 lengths of 26 1/2″ for horizontal sash, 2 lengths of 40 1/2″ for sides, 2 lengths of 30 1/2″ for top and bottom, and 3 lengths of 12 1/2″ for vertical sash.
4 squares, 5 1/2″, for carrot border corners

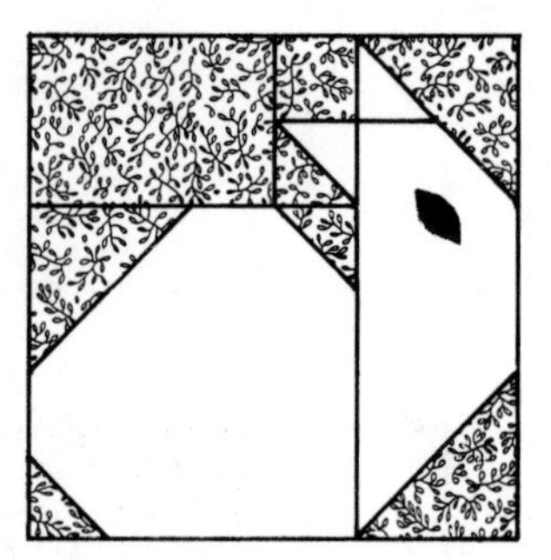

Bunny, 12″ block

From border background:
3 strips, 3 1/2″ wide
Subcut to 78D.
3 strips, 2 1/2″ wide
Subcut to 78E.
From fabric for carrots:
3 strips, 3 1/2″ wide
Subcut to 74D.
From fabric for carrot tops:
3 strips, 2 1/2″ wide
Subcut to 74E.

Sewing:

1. Following block piecing guide on page 54, sew 6 rabbit blocks.
2. Using Template C, follow directions for paper-piecing in Glossary of Techniques on page 62 to applique eyes to rabbits.
3. Following quilt diagram on page 53, sew blocks with sashing.
4. Make carrot strip.

Sew 15 carrot D to 16 background D, beginning and ending with background piece. Make 2. Sew 15 carrot top E to 16 background E, beginning and ending with background. Make 2. Join strip on long edge, centering point of green triangle on top of carrot.

Sew 22 carrot D to 23 background D, beginning and ending with background. Make 2. Sew 22 carrot top E to 23 background E, beginning and ending with background. Join strip on long edge. Add sashing corner squares to each end.

5. Sew short strips to top and bottom, and long strips to sides following quilt diagram on page 53.
6. Position backing, batting, and quilt top. Pin, baste, quilt, and bind according to directions in Glossary of Techniques on page 60-61.

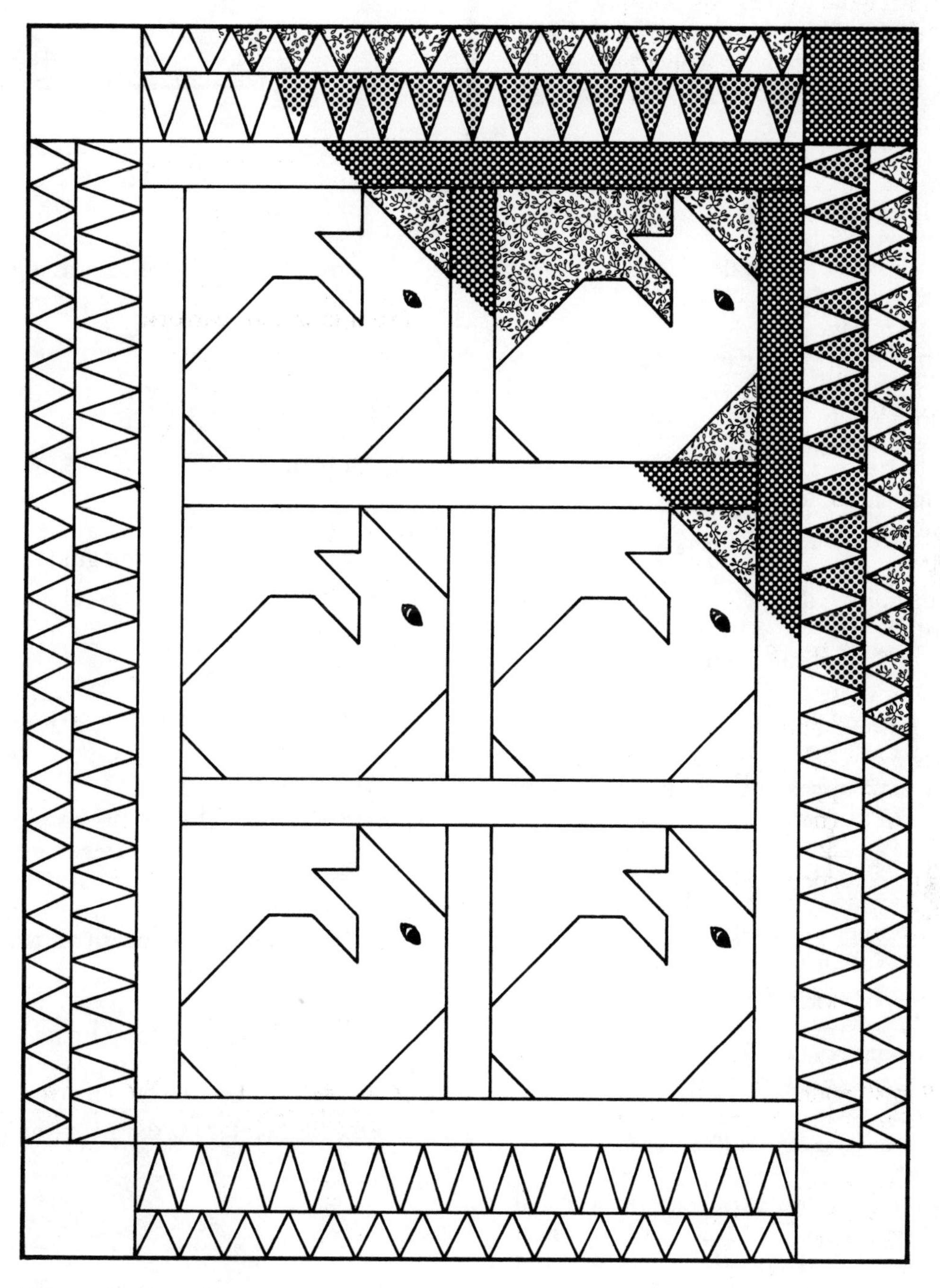

Bunny Lunch, 40″ x 54″

Whales in School

Color photo on page 29.

In this design, you may choose to reverse the whale pattern and have them "talking" to each other. Keeping in mind the name of this quilt, you can quilt this design in a variety of configurations. It looks like it truly is a school for whales, since the spouts appear to be spouting a variety of different ways!

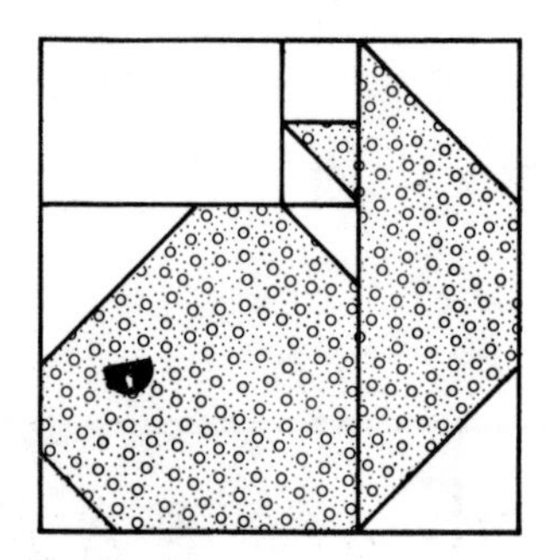

Whale, 12" block

Size: 45" x 56"

Materials: 45" wide fabric
1/4 yd. each of 6 prints for whales
1 2/3 yds. background and sashing
1/8 yd. or scraps for eyes
28 pieces, each 5" x 10", for fish border
1/2 yd. for binding
3 yds. for backing
45" x 60" baby quilt batting

Cutting: Strips are approximately 45" long, cut from selvage to selvage.

From each print for whales:
A: 1 square, 8 1/2" x 8 1/2". Use Cutting Template A in 2 opposite corners, and Cutting Template B in 1 corner.
B: 1 piece, 12 1/2" x 4 1/2". Use Cutting Template B in 2 corners on 1 long side.
E: 1 square, 2 7/8" x 2 7/8", cut diagonally to make 2 triangles (1 extra)
From background:
C: 2 strips, 4 7/8" wide
Subcut to 9 squares, 4 7/8" x 4 7/8", then cut diagonally to make 18 triangles.
D: 1 strip, 2 1/2" wide
Subcut to 6 squares, 2 1/2" x 2 1/2"
E: 1 strip, 2 7/8" wide
Subcut to 9 squares, 2 7/8" x 2 7/8", then cut diagonally to make 18 triangles.
F: 1 strip, 4 1/2" wide
Subcut to 6 lengths of 6 1/2" each.
4 strips, 2 1/2" wide
Subcut to 3 lengths of 12 1/2" each for vertical sashing, 2 lengths of 26 1/2" for horizontal sashing, and 2 lengths of 32 1/2" for top and bottom.
2 strips, 3 1/2" wide
Subcut to 2 lengths of 40 1/2" for sides.
3 strips, 3 1/4" wide, for fish border background.
Subcut to 14 squares, 3 1/4" x 3 1/4", then cut twice diagonally to make 56 small triangles.
2 strips, 2 7/8" wide for fish border background:
Subcut to 28 squares 2 7/8" x 2 7/8", then cut diagonally to make 56 large triangles.
5 strips, 2 1/2" wide, for last border
Subcut to 2 lengths of 45 1/2" for top and bottom, and 2 lengths of 55 1/2" for sides.
From print for eyes:
6 Template C plus 1/4" seam allowance
6 Template C from heavy paper
From scraps for fish border:
28 pieces, 4 1/2" x 6 1/2". Using Cutting Template A, cut 4 corners.
28 matching squares, 2 7/8" x 2 7/8", then cut diagonally to make 56 triangles for fish tail.
From binding print:
Cut 2 1/2" bias strips.

Sewing:
1. Following block piecing guide, sew 6 blocks.

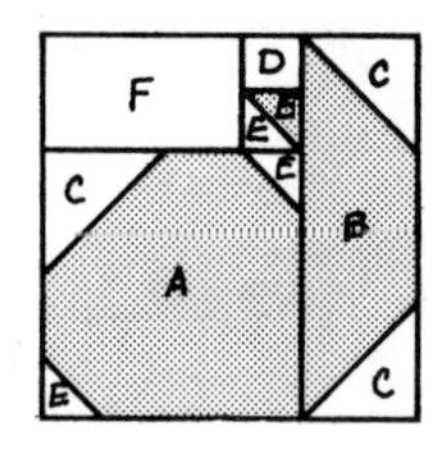

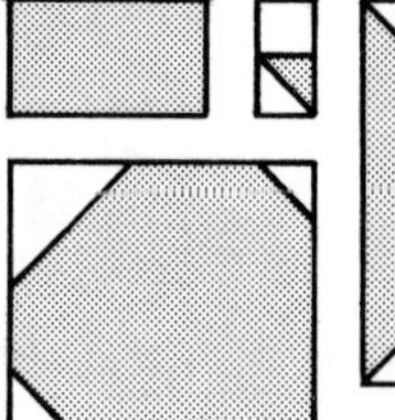

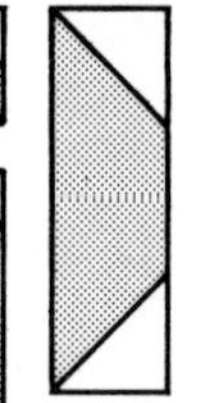

2. Cut 6 Eye Template C from paper and 6 from eye fabric adding 1/4" seam allowance. Following directions for paper-piecing in Glossary of Techniques on page 62, applique eyes.
3. Following quilt diagram on page 55, sew blocks with sashing for quilt top. Note that the side borders are wider than the top and bottom.
4. Sew 28 fish for border according to diagram.

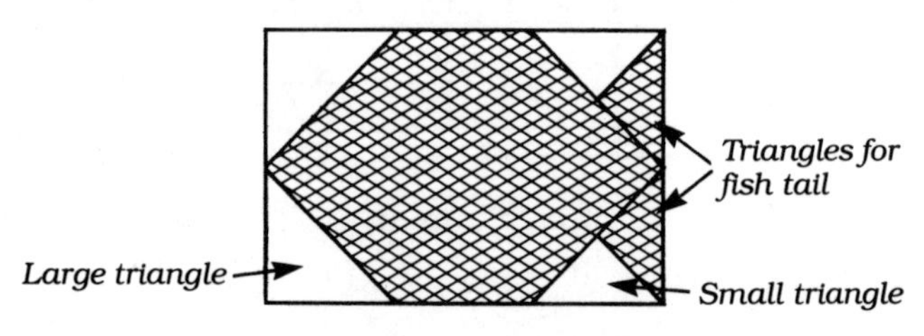

5. Following quilt piecing guide, join fish border in the same manner as bug border on page 28.
6. Sew border strips to sides, then top and bottom.
7. Position backing, batting, and quilt top. Pin, baste, quilt, and bind according to directions in Glossary of Techniques on pages 60-61.

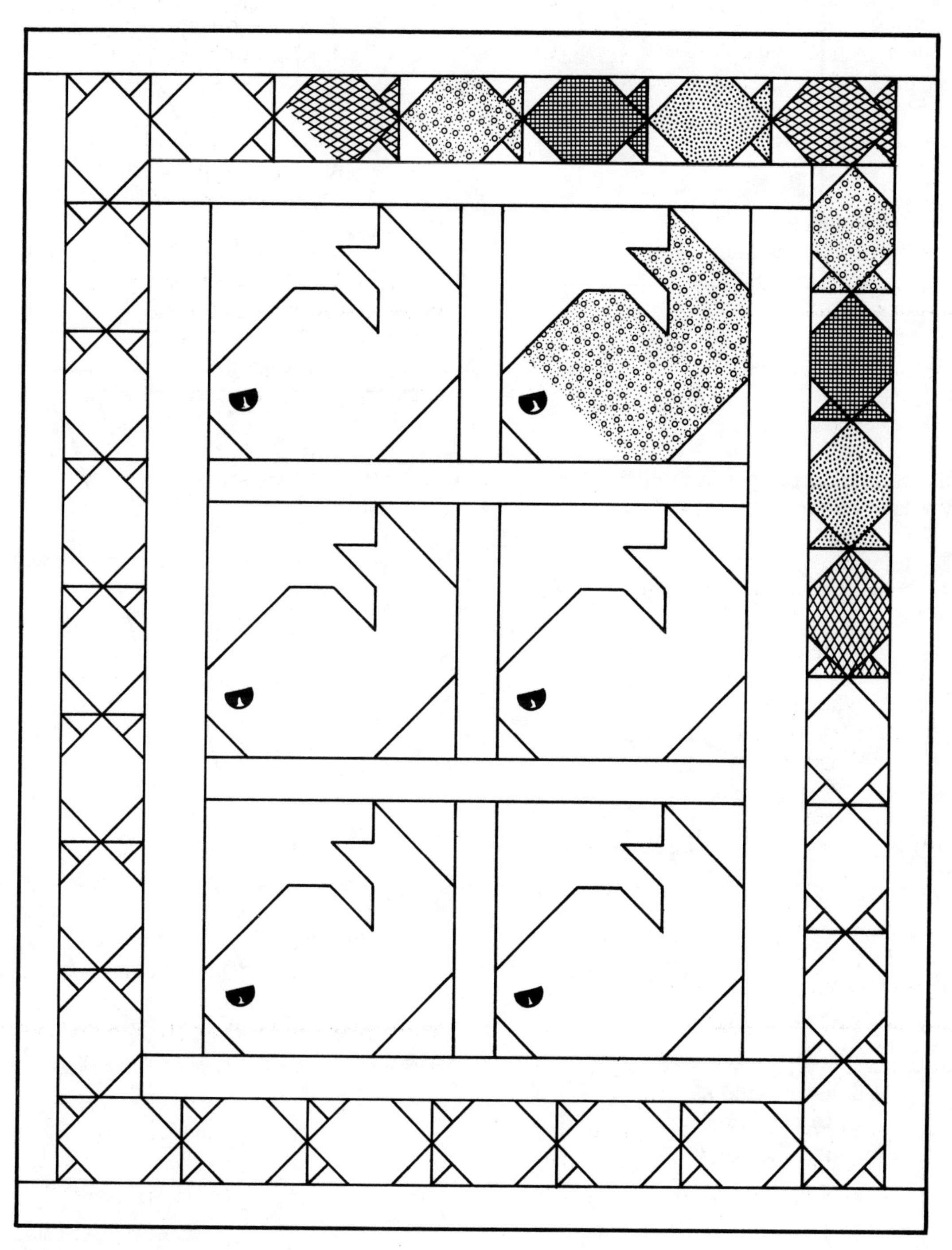

Whales in School, 45″ x 56″

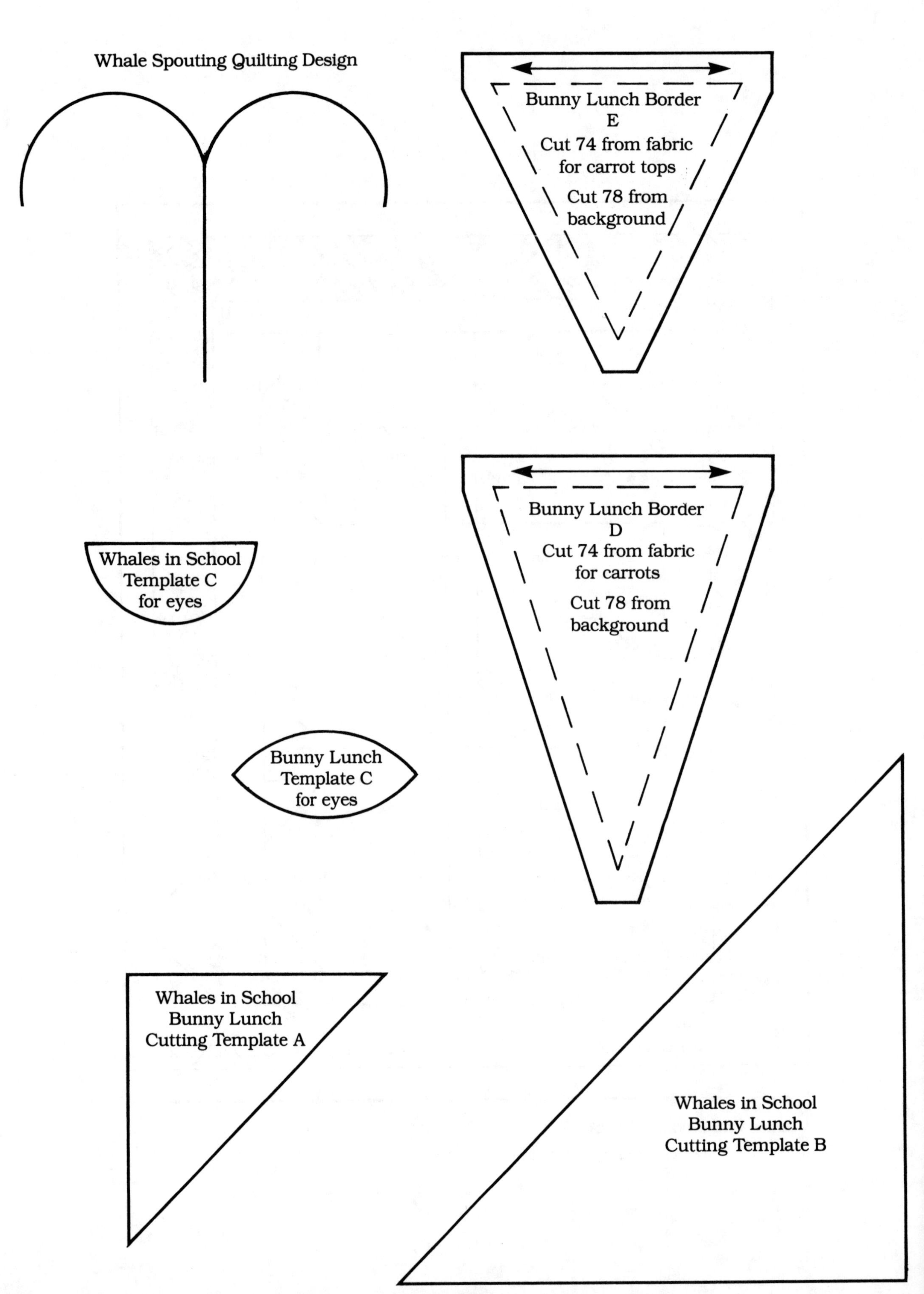
Whale Spouting Quilting Design
Bunny Lunch Border
E
Cut 74 from fabric
for carrot tops
Cut 78 from
background
Whales in School
Template C
for eyes
Bunny Lunch Border
D
Cut 74 from fabric
for carrots
Cut 78 from
background
Bunny Lunch
Template C
for eyes
Whales in School
Bunny Lunch
Cutting Template A
Whales in School
Bunny Lunch
Cutting Template B

Quilting Terms

Applique - to sew one piece of fabric on top of another by hand or machine. Example: eyes on an animal block.

Backing - fabric used for the underside or back of a quilt.

Baste - to take large stitches to hold quilt top, batting, and backing together so they won't shift while quilting.

Batting - a layer of cotton or polyester between the quilt top and backing that makes the quilt thick and "poofy"; purchased by the yard or in packages geared to the size of the bed.

Betweens - quilting needles.

Bias - a grainline that runs at a 45° angle to the lengthwise and crosswise grains and has considerable stretch.

Bias strip - a narrow length of fabric cut on the bias and used for binding or when a curved applique is needed.

Binding - fabric sewn on the outside edge of a quilt to enclose raw edges.

Block - a specified repetitive unit which is used to make a quilt top.

Block piecing guide - a diagram showing how template pieces are put together to make one block.

Coordinated prints - a group of different fabrics that look well together, sometimes produced by one manufacturer or designer.

Crosswise grain - threads that are woven from selvage to selvage and have some "give" to them.

Diagonal cut - squares of fabric cut from corner to corner of the square.

Grain - the direction that threads are woven.

Juvenile prints - printed fabric that has designs that appeal especially to children, like toys, small animals, etc.

Lengthwise grain - threads that are woven parallel to the selvage and have very little stretch.

Miter - borders of a quilt that meet at a 45° angle.

Multiple borders - more than one border, borders are named for the order they appear from the center of the quilt blocks, i.e. "First border" is the first border out from the center part of the quilt or block units.

Nondirectional fabric - where fabric design is the same both crosswise and lengthwise.

Novelty prints - printed fabric with unusual designs.

On point - quilt blocks set on the diagonal in a quilt.

Primary colors - red, yellow and blue

Quilt - (noun) two pieces of fabric enclosing a layer of batting with outer raw edges encased with binding; generally used for a bed covering or wall hanging.

Quilt - (verb) the act of taking tiny, even running stitches to hold a quilt together; quilting can be decorative and/or functional.

Quilt diagram - a diagram of a complete quilt to show placement of blocks, sashing, sashing squares, setting triangles and borders.

Rotary cutter - a round wheel with a sharp edge, like a pizza cutter, that cuts multiple layers of fabric; generally used with a plastic ruler or cutting guide.

Rotary mat - a special mat to use under a rotary cutter.

Rotary cutting guide - a thick plastic straight edge or ruler used to guide the rotary cutter and measure width of cuts.

Sashing - fabric strips between quilt blocks.

Seam allowance - 1/4" of fabric from stitching line to edge of fabric.

Selvage - the woven edges of a width of fabric.

Setting triangles - triangular shaped blocks of fabric placed along the outside edges of a diagonally set quilt top to make the edges even and straight.

Speed cutting - a technique used to quickly cut multiple pieces of fabric.

Speed piecing - various techniques to quickly put together a quilt top.

Strip - a piece of fabric cut on the crosswise grain a given number of inches from which squares or triangles are then cut.

Strip piecing - a technique of sewing long pieces of fabric together, then cutting crosswise into smaller units.

Subcut - to cut a strip of fabric or pieced fabric crosswise into a specified size.

Templates - paper or cardboard patterns used to cut fabric pieces for quilt blocks.

Texture - fabric that looks or is dimensional.

Thimble - a covering for the finger that pushes the needle when quilting.

Top - the upper side of a quilt or design.

Twist - a design that looks woven but really isn't.

Tying - taking heavy thread or yarn and making knots at intervals to hold a quilt together.

Glossary of Techniques

Borders

Most of the borders in this book are mitered. When there are several borders, the individual quilt instructions give directions for joining the strips at the short ends and then sewing the long edges together to form a long strip. For all other borders, use the following instructions and diagrams.

1. Turn under at a 45° angle and press one end of strip, leaving a 1/2″ allowance. Cut.
2. Place a pin 1/4″ from edge on fold.
3. From this pin, measure the finished length of quilt side.
4. Place another pin at this point and turn under at a 45° angle, leaving 1/2″ allowance and cut.
5. Make 2 strips for top and bottom of quilt top and 2 strips for sides.
6. With right sides together, match borders according to diagram. Pin in place at beginning and end of seam line.

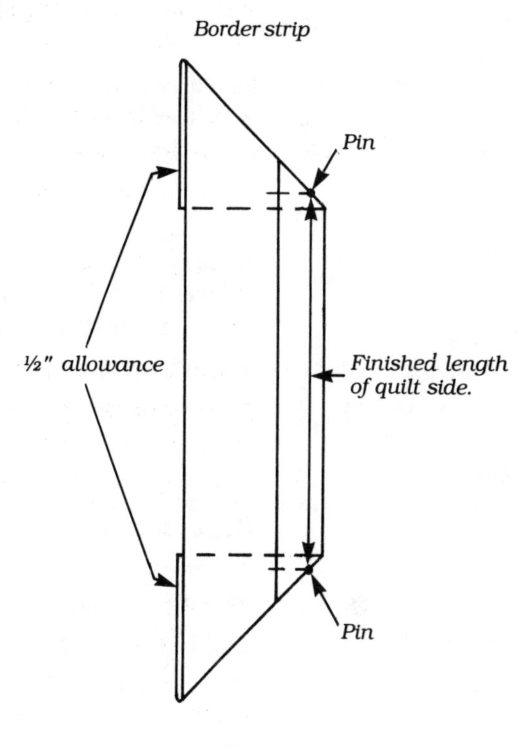

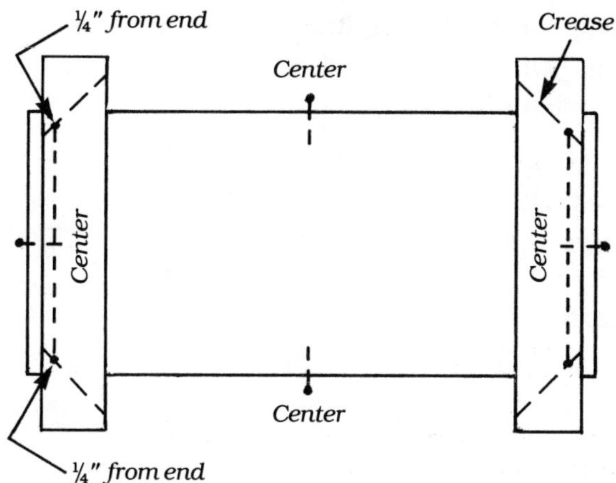
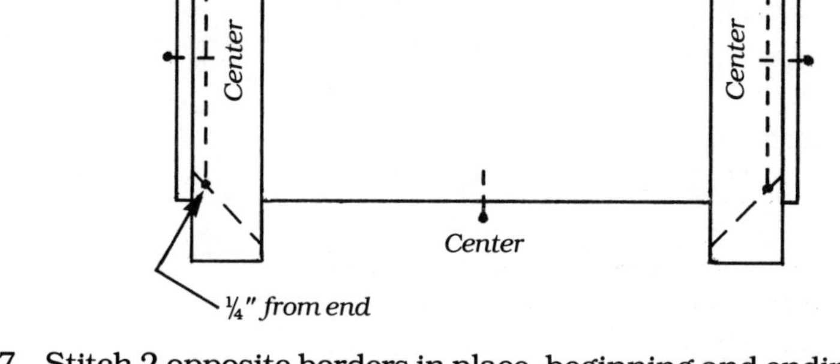

7. Stitch 2 opposite borders in place, beginning and ending seams at the pin.
8. Press seams flat with seam allowances toward the borders.
9. Repeat with remaining 2 borders. (Seams will begin and end at the end of the 2 previously stitched border seams.)
10. Working on one corner at a time, adjust folds to form a mitered corner, using the extra 1/2″ to adjust fold line if necessary.
11. On right side, place a piece of masking tape over folded seam to hold in place.
12. From wrong side, sew on fold line to make mitered corner. Remove masking tape, trim seam, and press open.

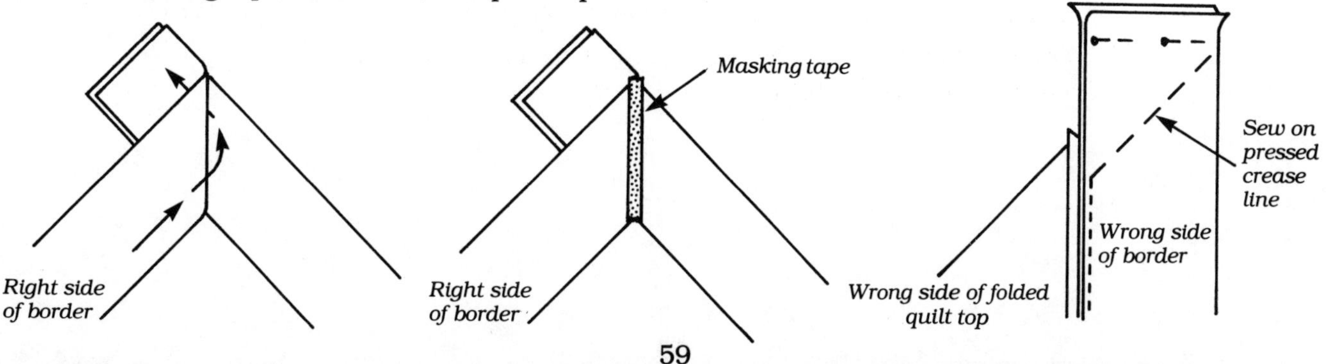

Quilting Procedure

Position backing, batting, and top:

Tape the backing piece to floor or table, wrong side up. Lay batting piece on top and smooth out. Carefully place top, right side up, over batting, making sure the backing and batting extend beyond the top several inches. Working from the center, smooth out with hands.

To determine size of quilt batting needed, add 4″ to length and 4″ to width measurement of quilt top. This gives a generous allowance on all four sides of the quilt.

Pin:

Starting at center of quilt, pin all 3 layers together with quilting pins. Continue pinning at 8-10″ intervals as shown in diagram.

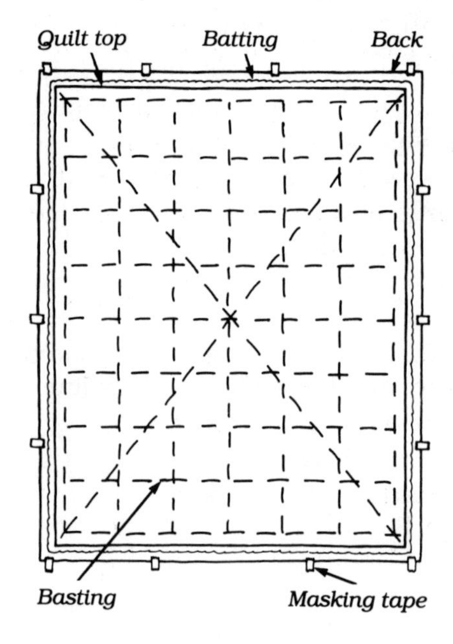

Baste:

Starting at center and working out, baste in a 4″ grid over entire quilt, smoothing out with hands as needed.

Quilt:

Your quilt is now ready to put in a hoop or on a quilt frame. Start at center and quilt out to edges, moving hoop or frame as needed. Using quilting thread and needle, take tiny running stitches. Check back of quilt frequently to be sure the needle goes all the way through the batting and backing.

My personal preference for quilting is to use an old-fashioned quilt frame, where the quilt is put flat on the frame, stretched taut, and rolled from both ends when quilted. This kind of frame is made from four 1 x 4's.

1. Tack a narrow cloth strip to one long side of each board and use C-clamps in the 4 corners.

2. Pin backing to each of two end pieces; stretch out and use other pieces for sides; clamp taut.

3. Place frame on the backs of four chairs. Pin backing to side pieces. Make sure the four corners are square and backing is taut without ripples.

4. Roll out batting on top. Carefully place pieced top on batting. Stretch and pin at edges as necessary.

5. Quilt from each end in as far as comfortable, about 12″. Then release clamps, turn end piece under, clamp, and quilt another strip across until center of quilt is reached from both ends. Unwind and remove from frame.

This method eliminates basting and ensures a pucker-free back; however, space is needed to set it up and it is not portable. For most baby quilts, quilting in a hoop is easier.

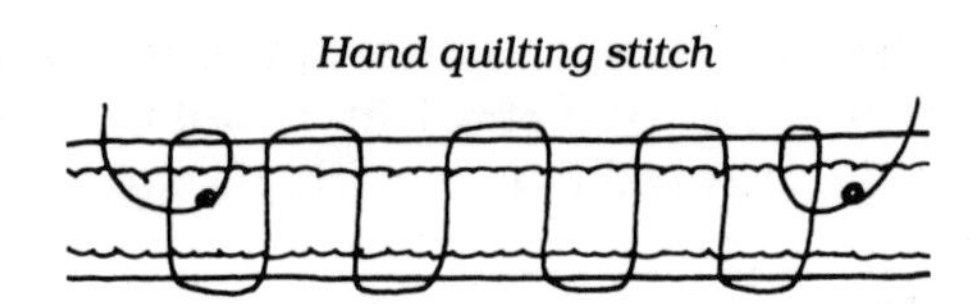

Most of the designs in this book were quilted "in the ditch," which means the stitches were made very close to the quilt top seam lines. Some of the designs were marked with a water erasable pen, while others were put on with 1/4" masking tape. Machine quilting with invisible thread was used on most of the quilts. I find that this method is quicker and is very practical for a quilt that must be washed a lot. However, the thread has yet to withstand the test of time as to how well it will wear.

I find that where a design needs to be traced onto a block, it is generally easier to trace it on before the top is sewn together. This was the case in the Irish Bear Chain.

If you choose to tie your quilt, use embroidery floss, perle cotton, or lightweight yarn. With double thread, tie at 4-6" intervals in a square knot. You may also use 1/16" ribbon for a special effect.

Remember that you need to quilt around the part of the design you wish to stand out most to make it poofy. Look at your design and select the method that is easiest for you. One nice thing about the art of quilting is that there is generally more than one way to do each step, which leaves the door open for experimenting.

Binding

1. To find the true bias, bring one corner of fabric up to opposite corner and press. Cut on press line.
2. Measure and cut 2 1/2" bias strips on this line. Seam ends to make one long strip. Fold, matching raw edges. Press.
3. Starting along one side of quilt, match binding and quilt top edge. Batting and backing will extend beyond the 1/4" seam allowance. Using a 1/4" seam allowance, stitch to within 1/4" of corner edge, backstitch, and remove from machine.
4. Fold binding away from corner at a 90° angle. Bottom edge of binding and quilt will be parallel. Finger press fold and carefully flip binding back, making a fold at edge of right side.

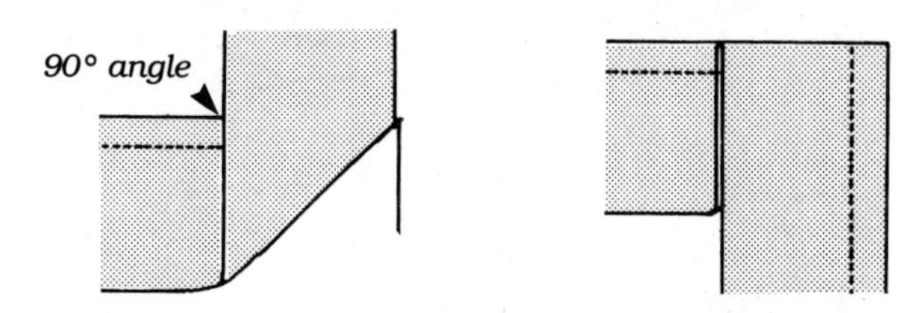

5. Start stitching at edge of fabric and continue down side. Repeat for other three corners. Trim raw edges to 1/2". This extra "poof" from batting and backing will fill out the binding, making it firm and full. It also increases wear.
6. Hand stitch to back of quilt, carefully turning in binding to make a miter. It will fall in place as you do it.

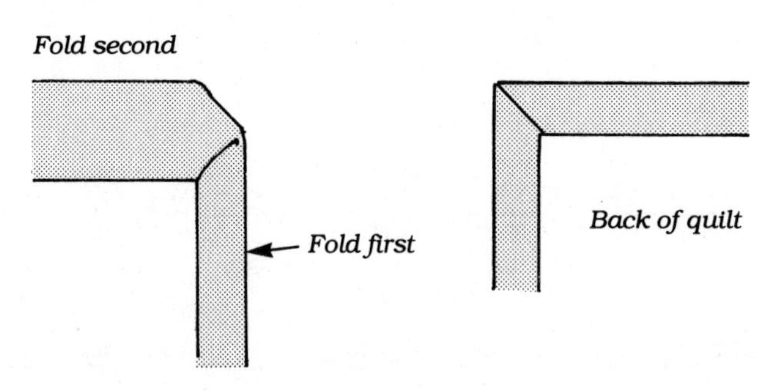

Marking bias strips

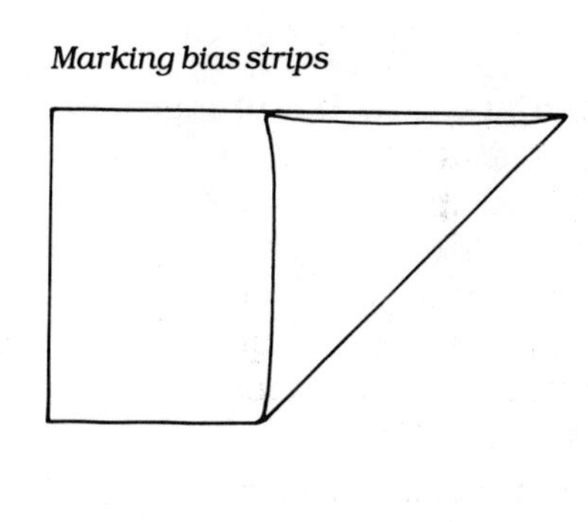

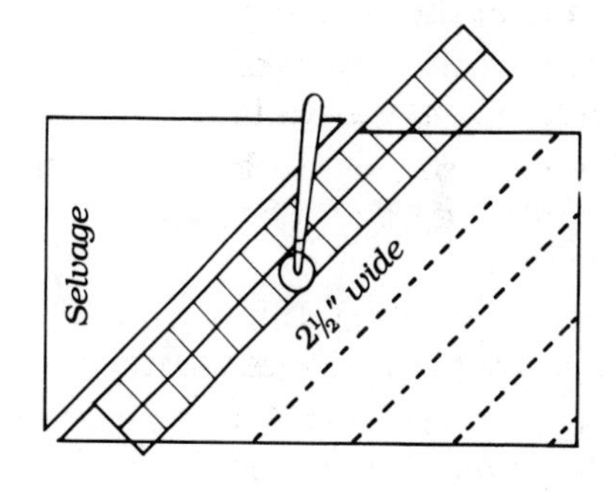

Joining bias strips

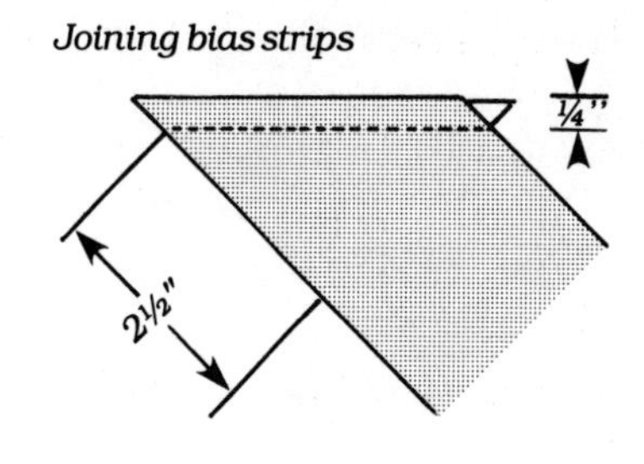

Paper-Piecing Applique

Applique is used on several quilts in this book. You may applique by hand or machine. I prefer using a technique called paper-piecing.

1. Make templates for all pattern pieces from construction paper or medium-weight bond paper. Do not add seam allowance.

2. Place templates on fabric and pin. Add 1/4″ around all edges of template and cut.

3. Fold 1/4″ seam allowance over template. You may fold fabric towards you or away from you, whichever way is most comfortable for you. Baste fabric to template, using a running stitch and sewing through the paper.

4. Clip inner curves and indentations, gently stretching fabric.

5. On outer curves, ease in fullness, using a small running stitch to gather the fabric. Do not sew through paper on outer curves. The basting stitches that go through the paper on either end of the outer curve will hold the fabric to the paper.

6. Baste all fabric pieces to paper. Do not use knots after the last basting stitches, since the basting stitches and paper must be removed in a later step.

7. Press all fabric pieces, easing fabric to ensure that bumpy edges are not created during pressing.

8. Applique fabric pieces to background, using a small blind stitch and matching thread. Stitches should be fairly close together. When applique is completed, turn block to wrong side and carefully cut away background fabric under the applique piece, leaving 1/4″ seam allowance. Remove basting thread from applique piece, and paper will come out easily. This leaves one less fabric layer to quilt.

Pin paper to fabric.

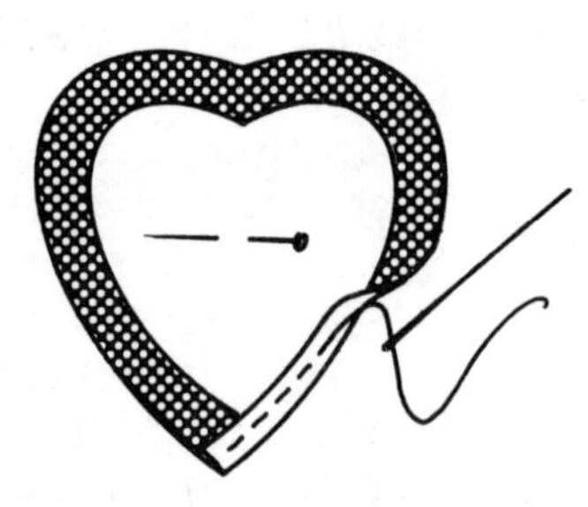

Baste fabric to paper, sewing through paper.

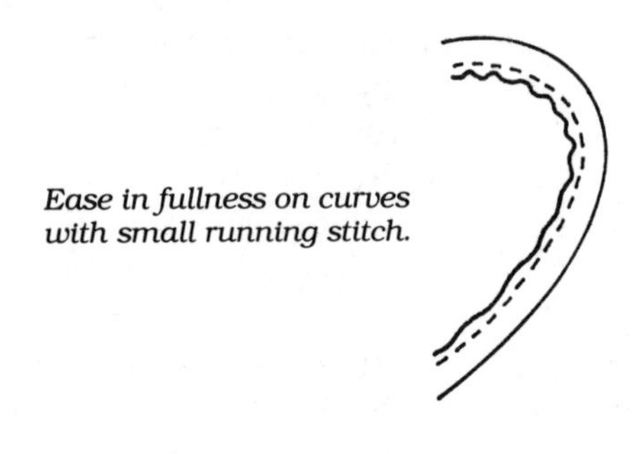

Ease in fullness on curves with small running stitch.

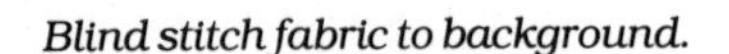

Blind stitch fabric to background.

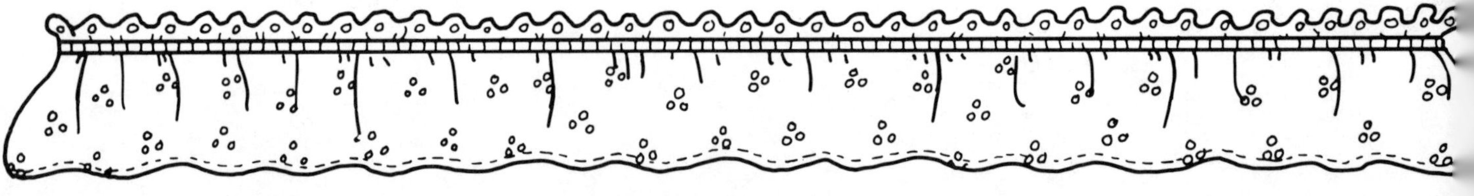

Labels

When your quilt is finished, make a label for the back, giving the name of the quilt, the person who made and quilted it, date completed, owner of quilt, and city and state where made. Include any other pertinent information, such as a specific occasion or special fabrics. You may wish to include baby's birth weight, date, place, etc. These labels can be as fancy or as simple as you desire. You can type on a piece of muslin, do embroidery, or cross-stitch.

There are so many ways of making a quilt, no one way is necessarily "correct." After 32 years of quilting, I am still discovering new ways and learning new techniques. Some methods make it easier, may look better, or take less time. Experiment with ideas until you find one that is just right for you. Above all, enjoy what you are doing and be proud of it!

Happy Baby Quilting!

RAINBOW KITES
DESIGNED, PIECED &
QUILTED BY
CAROLANN M PALMER for
BABY QUILTS FROM
© 1988 GRANDMA
42 x 52

Meet the Author

Carolann Palmer, quilt teacher and designer, is an enthused and excited quilter who is eager to share her ideas with others. Carolann made her first quilt over 30 years ago and has since made well over a hundred; 90 of these were baby quilts for friends and family. She has sewn everything from baby clothes and crib quilts to wedding dresses for her grown daughters.

Carolann receives much satisfaction from sharing her quilting skills and enthusiasm. She is the author of Branching Out—Tree Quilts, also published by That Patchwork Place, Inc. She is an active member of her quilt guild, Quilter's Anonymous, of which she is a past president. Carolann is active in church activities and likes to cook, camp, and enjoy the outdoors of the Pacific Northwest.

THAT PATCHWORK PLACE PUBLICATIONS

Back To Square One by Nancy J. Martin
Bearwear by Nancy J. Martin
Branching Out - Tree Quilts by Carolann Palmer
Cathedral Window - A New View by Mary Ryder Kline
Christmas Classics by Sue Saltkill
Christmas Memories - A Folk Art Celebration by Nancy J. Martin
Christmas Quilts by Marsha McCloskey
Copy Art for Quilters by Nancy J. Martin
Dozen Variables by Marsha McCloskey and Nancy J. Martin
Feathered Star Quilts by Marsha McCloskey
Feathered Star Sampler by Marsha McCloskey
Happy Endings - Finishing the Edges of Your Quilt by Mimi Dietrich
Holiday Happenings by Christal Carter
Housing Projects by Nancy J. Martin
Make a Medallion by Kathy Cook
More Template-Free Quiltmaking by Trudie Hughes
My Mother's Quilts: Designs from the Thirties by Sara Nephew
Pieces of the Past by Nancy J. Martin
Projects for Blocks and Borders by Marsha McCloskey
Quilter's Christmas by Nancyann Twelker
Quilts From a Different Angle by Sara Nephew
Sew Special by Susan A. Grosskopf
Small Quilts by Marsha McCloskey
Stencil Patch by Nancy J. Martin
Template-Free Quiltmaking by Trudie Hughes
Wall Quilts by Marsha McCloskey

For more information, send $2 for our color catalog to That Patchwork Place, Inc., P.O. Box 118, Bothell, WA 98041-0118. Many titles available at your local quilt shop.